Refugees

The Magix Series

Book One

Written by

P. Ryall

Refugees

Refugees

P. Ryall

Copyright © 2025, P. Ryall

ISBN:

eBook: 978-1-923493-72-8
Paperback: 978-1-923493-73-5
Hardback: 978-1-923493-74-2

All Rights Reserved. This book may not be reproduced, transmitted, or stored in whole or part in any means, including graphic, electronic, or mechanical without the express written consent of the publisher except in the case of brief quotations embodied in critical articles and reviews.

Acknowledgements

A huge thank you to my family and beta reading team, for listening to me talk about Refugees endlessly.

For my children, you are my everything.

Danielle, my epic editor. Thank you for rescuing me when everything that could go wrong did, and for all the incredible help you've given me since. I am eternally grateful and look forward to working with you again.

And for my cat, Mr Binx. He sits with me daily and makes sure I am doing my job.

Refugees

The Huntowra are coming...

They want to destroy all life, everywhere.

A war has been brewing for centuries and forced thousands from their homes. Now they're all refugees, trying to piece their lives back together. They quickly become friends with the inhabitants of their temporary home and form an alliance with them in the coming battle. Can they stop the Huntowra before it's too late? Or will they all fall?

When a member of the Elite Five, the fiercest of all the Huntowra, is caught, he accidentally lets some new information slip. The queens, who were the most lethal of all, feared another queen. One that nobody knew existed. Until now.

Friends will fight, families will be united, and bonds of brotherhood will form.

This is the beginning.

P. Ryall

Table of Contents

Acknowledgements iii

Chapter 1 1

Chapter 2 7

Chapter 3 9

Chapter 4 12

Chapter 5 19

Chapter 6 23

Chapter 7 28

Chapter 8 36

Chapter 9 44

Chapter 10 49

Chapter 11 52

Chapter 12 55

Chapter 13 59

Chapter 14 63

Chapter 15 66

Chapter 16 69

Refugees

Chapter 17	73
Chapter 18	77
Chapter 19	79
Chapter 20	82
Chapter 21	85
Chapter 22	88
Chapter 23	96
Chapter 24	106
Chapter 25	108
Chapter 26	111
Chapter 27	117
Chapter 28	124
Chapter 29	130
Chapter 30	137
Chapter 31	144
Chapter 32	150
Chapter 33	159
Chapter 34	170
Chapter 35	180

Chapter 36	190
Chapter 37	199
Chapter 38	204
Chapter 39	210
Chapter 40	216
Chapter 41	222
About the Author	229

P. Ryall

Chapter 1

Twenty-Five years ago

Meakra was a beautiful world. It had gigantic cities with grand buildings everywhere and cobbled streets that lay so neatly it appeared as though magix had created them. Of course, there were several beautiful worlds in the universe. The closest and most similar was Haven. The people of Haven were called Talgra and the people from Meakra known as Whistler (pronounced wish-la). They had long been friends, sharing in each other's glories and hardships. Feeling each other's pain and passions. The primary difference between the Talgra and the Whistler was that the Talgra had stripes on their bodies that came and went, and their hair could change colour with their moods. The stripes were birthmarks that faded and reappeared at will—the result of an extra gene—but their ability to change their hair colour with emotions was all magix. Each Talgra had unique colours for their different emotions. Haven and Meakra—along with one other world, Helios—had very large and strong armies, so they helped other worlds when they could, making them fairly popular among the other beings.

But not everything was well. The entire universe was preparing for an all-out war with the Huntowra, and tensions with them were reaching fever pitch. This had been brewing for many hundreds of years, since the Huntowra declared that they were the only species worth existing. They weren't interested

Refugees

in sharing worlds with us, nor did they care how brutally they slaughtered us; they only cared for destruction. The way they moved and behaved was like a plague of demons.

Nobody was sure exactly why it had happened, but the Huntowra had gotten sick, and many died. Those who survived developed ridges on their faces and blotches of coppery skin all over their bodies. They also developed severe personality problems, going from the kind and caring beings they were to mass murderers. Subsequent generations underwent changes before they even emerged into their world. Many had believed they were cursed, but now it was widely known that some form of viral infection had caused the mutation. This was a sickness that altered the very genetics of an entire species, and it had spread rapidly, destroying them within five decades.

It was unlikely that we would ever know for sure where, or how, it had started, but some senior council officials were working with healers to try and pinpoint a cause, allowing us to better understand them—their aggression anyway. Perhaps we could slow them down, at least. There was no hope for a cure, but it had provided our healers with a much-needed distraction from the raging feud.

We all had magix; it usually showed itself briefly at birth and was then dormant until around twelve years old. When the magix resurfaced, each being was asked to step into the magix ring so they could receive their full power. The ring assessed your abilities, and showed your areas of strengths, which indicated what work you were best suited to. For example, if you were chosen for the warriors' life, they sent you to live in the training grounds to get to know your fellow warriors intimately—they would become like your second family. It was an honour, everyone's idea of a dream job. It was possible to change callings; but it rarely happened.

The gender of a being meant nothing to the ring—it was indiscriminate and therefore useful for reading a being's potential.

There were instances where a youngling had power that did not regress, a serious threat. The young had no control over the magix inside them, which meant that a tantrum could destroy whole towns. So, many centuries ago, it was decided that these children needed to be cast out into the Qualterra, a barren world. These children were referred to as the forbidden children, and the few who survived and returned were somewhat the outcasts in society, but they seemed happy enough and there were always jobs for them to do. They still contributed to society, but there were limitations—they could never be members of council, never achieve above a captain status as a warrior, and interplanetary travel was monitored closely, for safety reasons. We didn't understand yet why their magix had never regressed, but there were serious concerns about the magix going out of control and causing harm to both the being and others nearby.

There were also quite a few worlds out there that had no idea of our existence. Some worlds had no magix whatsoever, which was just baffling. Others had magix and were too shy to travel, like the Vispers. They were powerful healers and loved observing other species, eagerly taking note of every action. Their keen interest in other species surprised the council, which was made from high ranking government members of many worlds, given their inherent shyness, but they did tend to stay well back and out of sight if possible—not easy given that they glowed a bright, pale blue and had very large catlike eyes.

Very rarely a youngling would come into existence that

Refugees

was destined to change everything, and in the case of the Whistler, there had long been a legend, it came from one of the most powerful seers in their history, she spoke of a youngling with immense magix, like nothing ever seen before, and it made everyone nervous. When this youngling reached adult status, he or she would be the most powerful being that had ever existed. There was another legend linked to this one, scrawled by other seers, but it was too obscure to understand. They knew for sure that they'd know the precious child by the magix ring, which would perform magix never before witnessed.

The elders on the council, the cave dragons, the Talgra, and even the Vispers were all strategizing ways to ensure that nobody would come to harm. They assumed that the magix would not recede. This child would be pivotal in the war against the Huntowra, so they needed to guarantee his or her survival and safety. To that end, they'd all come up with clever ways of restricting power, minimising the impact of power explosions, and literally stopping the forbidden children from blowing apart from the intensity of the eruptions. They created several safety towers to reduce the accidental sparks, sort of like lightning striking a metal tower. They also created a safety barrier, ten layers of shielding that went around the magix ring and platform. Our ways were changing, and our peoples flourishing.

There were new amulets, and fine chains called power bands, that wrapped around the body and sucked away excess power, releasing a sedative, to relax the being when in great distress. They worked better than anyone could have ever imagined. When the being reached a more mature level, they removed the band in the magix ring and the being then received their full power. Taking the power bands off needed special training to; it could be dangerous if done improperly.

The inventor of the power bands was an incredibly devoted father and loving husband, who also happened to be royalty, next in line to inherit his world and all its responsibilities. His name is Matthew. He and his lovely wife Amanda had a son Daemon and a daughter Lilah. They lived on the outskirts of the palace grounds, right near the village in a small cottage. The entire area was rich with native plants and flowers, some protective and some just for decoration or pretty scents. They were close friends with a couple from Haven, and the friends often got together. Allen and Camilla had two sons the same age as Daemon, Ethan and Peter, along with eleven older sons. Peter, Ethan and Lilah were best friends; but Peter and Lilah had a unique magix connection from the moment she had been born. He held her moments after she had been born, and an eternal bracelet appeared on both the children's left arms, linking the two souls together for all eternity. This was a gesture so rare and powerful that only twenty or so beings had been able to create them in all the known history of our worlds. Peter clearly had not performed the magix, so the bracelet had to have come from the new-born baby girl.

Word spread unbelievably fast, and people started to whisper about her. Her parents were sure it was just a fluke, but then strange things started happening—like levitation, or Peter mysteriously appearing out of nowhere at odd hours. And then, a tree with silver berries as large as apples sprang up early one cold morning, shaking the ground and making a sound like thunder. Matt and Amanda had rushed outside to find Peter holding the infant, staring at the tree in some kind of trance. The tree—and the children—were surrounded by a barrier, which meant that no one could intervene, and several of the silver berries dissolved into silvery ribbons and were absorbed by the infant. Although toxic to everyone else, they appeared to be her

Refugees

natural food source.

Finally, when Peter started insisting that she understood everything around her and that she was communicating with him, her worried parents demanded that she be put in the ring. It was almost completely unheard of to test a youngling so soon after birth, but after much discussion with the council of elders, they placed the sleepy youngling in the ring with the entire council watching on, along with representatives of many other worlds.

Then the ring did something unexpected. First, it magicked the baby over to the Kalix ring—a more powerful and dangerous magix ring—then it played a lullaby, and all the symbols lit up at once. The area trembled and an enormous earthquake cracked the ground open all around the tiny infant, who yawned casually. A large symbol rose above her head: flaming wings that twisted and twirled fifty feet in the air, glowing so brightly it even lit the palace front, and that was over six kilometres away. The masses of people and other assorted beings all gasped, and screams rang out.

This was the youngling. It had to be.

Chapter 2

As the years slowly moved forward, Lilah grew like any other youngling. Her beautiful chocolate curls floated about her heart-shaped face, and her inky green eyes were cat-like slits that seemed to glow slightly. She was small for her age and preferred to speak using telepathy. There were other differences, of course—some of them very obvious—but she tried her best to pretend to be just like other little girls. She was often teased because she was special, and many adults were frightened of her.

She was indulgent with her dear ones and loved Peter more than anything else in the universe. He, of course, felt the same way, but hid his own differences better—partly because he had twelve older brothers who commanded their mother's attention, and partly because he simply wasn't as advanced as her. Yet. Nobody knew just how special he was, but one day they would all understand. Until then, it was one of their secrets, and nobody would make her tell it until he was ready for them to know.

Which was why she hadn't been able to explain to her daddy why she'd gone to Peter's world to visit him when he was grounded. Even though nobody had said *she* couldn't visit *him*, nor told her she wasn't allowed to portal on her own, they were very upset, and now she was grounded too. She hated not seeing her Peter and needed to know he was okay, so she reached out to him with her mind. He was sad, but when he sensed her presence, he cheered up. They could see through

Refugees

each other's eyes and hear what the other heard, and they spent an entire week in their bedrooms just being connected. It was a little weird having his memories and thoughts and feelings as well as her own, but they enjoyed being so bound to each other. It was comforting and helped ease their loneliness.

Still, Peter told no one and warned her that the adults would likely be very scared if they knew she could connect at will and over such a great distance. For one thing, it meant her magix was actually growing, which had never happened before. And for another, they would likely figure out a way to stop her from using her ability. Her daddy and the elders had already insisted she have power bands, even though they felt like they were suffocating her and she'd never even *had* a tantrum. But they said the other children would feel better if she was treated the same as them, and she'd caved. They were her dear ones, after all, and she loved every one of them.

The only time she felt relief from the bands was when she absorbed the berries from her tree. It didn't behave as any other tree did; this one was always in fruit and when she was near, it gleamed with its bright colours and silver berries, which shone brightly. When she was off on other worlds, though, the tree wilted a bit and was less vibrant. Even the berries dulled. This always corrected itself when she returned to her world, so she didn't worry too much. This was a very special tree, it gave her sustenance and offered her and Peter a safe and quiet place to enjoy each other's company. Ethan sometimes played with them to, but he mostly preferred to run around, chasing his older brothers.

Chapter 3

One cool evening in a quiet street, while families cooked their evening meals and chatted to each other happily, two little girls were playing dolls, as they had many times before. The smaller girl was listening intently while the older girl told a joke, when, without warning, a portal opened and five beings appeared on the street. They immediately headed down the street towards the two girls, moving as quietly as possible.

Nosk, the leader of this group of Huntowra, had been ordered by their master to get rid of a powerful child. If she reached adulthood, she would be too strong, and they would surely lose the battle and with it, the war.

Today, it would begin. With the slain youngling's blood on his hands, he would call forth the armada of Huntowra brothers waiting to slaughter every being on this wretched planet. And from here, every other planet in the alliance would fall, one by one, the strongest first. The attack had already been planned; this was just a distraction to keep them from banding together.

Nosk and his brothers spread their wings in preparation for the fight. They chuckled at how easy it had been so far. The girls turned and froze, the elder in fear, but the small one only seemed impatient. Rather odd for a youngling, but it didn't matter much to him; he had no offspring and never would. The elder girl had muddy brown hair plaited to her waist and her eyes were like river water, a greyish blue. Common in every

Refugees

sense, but a flicker of power deep inside suggested that she might be a powerful adult.

The tiny imp's chocolate curls moved in the breeze like they had a life of their own. Her cat-like eyes were a strange green colour and almost glowed. Though she seemed like any other youngling at first, this little beast had magix and was controlling it, hiding her strength from those around her. That she could contain it this way only proved how powerful she would be if allowed to reach adulthood. She was little more than a toddler, with maybe five years of life. Sickened, he snarled viciously as he grabbed the offensive little meat-sack and turned to leave.

He'd just registered that she neither fought nor spoke when the elder girl screamed and flailed with her fists, trying desperately to free the smaller one. His brother Leinad landed a sharp kick to the whining brat's gut, and the next second, she had full armour and a sword. Should he kill her too? No. He shook his head. She could wait for another day, and he would personally see to it that the day came. The girl swung her sword blindly, and Leinad screeched in fury, grabbing at his side. The little monster had struck a serious blow, but they still left with minimal fuss. An easy victory.

Now all they had to do was kill the child—and quickly, so they could begin this war in earnest, putting an end to the boredom of hiding and the frustration of small scuffles. Throwing the little beast from a great height into a horde of Shrogan was the surest way of killing her. Even if she survived the fall, the Shrogan would tear her apart. His master would be happy. She was the most vicious creature he'd ever encountered but had managed to get abnormally close to key members of the alliance over the years she'd been embedded there. An image came to him of the sickening disguise she wore, and the little beast gasped. Clearly, he'd hurt it. He nearly smiled.

They made their way into the Qualterra and found a densely populated area of Shrogan. Though the immortal beasts also sensed power, they were dim-witted and spent their time ripping each other apart. As Nosk threw the beastly youngling in amongst them, Leinad started to pant. A thick stream of blood poured from his side, and he almost fell. Furious, Nosk caught him. How could a worthless little runt have caused this amount of damage to his brother?

He needed to get him back to their encampment so he could heal him. At least the little monster who'd done this would die in screaming agony, and they would never have to fear the child who could destroy them all again.

Chapter 4

Present day

The Qualterra was a complete wasteland. The hordes of Shrogan that dwelled there were horrible. They smelled and constantly fought with each other and anyone else unfortunate enough go there. The shrubby trees looked more like slime-covered sticks, poking out from cave walls and cliff faces. The storms in Qualterra were horrible too. They had rain like acid that lasted for days. During the wet season, it often flooded, and the temperatures were freezing. The Forbidden Ones used to get sent to the Qualterra, but now with Matt's power bands, there was no need.

About twenty-five years ago, several worlds were attacked and suffered severe damage in the war with the Huntowra. It had forced thousands to leave their homes while repairs were carried out, and they had all found refuge on a safe world out of the Huntowra's reach.

It was an insignificant planet with no magix. Earth. The people were a strange and paranoid species, often brutal and almost always at war with themselves. But they were also targets for the Huntowra, so in return for safe refuge, they joined the alliance. Now, several years after the first encounter, they had become friends.

Peter and his brother Jeff were scouting the Qualterra, looking for a doorway, sealed with magix and hidden somewhere. That wasn't the only reason to search this place, though; there were other things they hoped to find. Jeff was a quiet man. His empathic nature meant he felt everything, including his brother's turbulent emotions. He said nothing, though, and Peter was grateful for it. They walked in silence, though normally they would've both been laughing and chatting.

Peter had been a warrior since he was twelve years old. He'd dreamed of being the strongest, smartest, and best warrior out there, but had soon learnt that he was far from those things. One day when training with his brothers, he'd sent himself here by accident. It was an innocent mistake, one that could have…probably should have killed him. He hadn't been focused enough, he was thinking of Lilah, and wham…he was sent through a portal. There was no Lilah waiting for him, but he always felt as though she was near.

The feeling of her presence had saved Peter's life that day—because he'd been blown apart but then, somehow, healed. The golden chains attached to the eternal bracelet had covered his entire body and instantly pulled him back together, healing his wounds in the process. It had been a close call, and he was severely winded and in shock, defenceless. A horde of Shrogan thundered toward him as he struggled to breathe, no doubt intent on killing him.

He hadn't known even the most basic barrier spell at that age, but there'd been an enormous surge of magix followed by a flash of green, and he'd blacked out. When Peter woke, the Shrogan were gone, but a girl was there. She spoke to him, and the sheer power in her quiet voice blew him away. She glowed, and her snow-white hair moved on its own. Her eyes were like fire, but a milky film covered them so they looked almost

Refugees

completely white.

Something about her presence made Peter feel as though he'd always known her, yet he didn't. Just being near her made him feel like the air was charged and ready to explode into a billion pieces, but it was oddly comforting. He'd sensed that, somehow, she was protecting him. Everyone had later insisted she had to have been an illusion—his mind trying to rationalise what had happened—but it had seemed so real.

Peter had woken in a small cave littered with bones with paintings all over the walls. There was even a small river flowing through it. The Shrogan dwelled in the caves, but this had felt a little different. Safer, somehow.

He struggled against the onslaught of memories and tried to refocus on the present. Recently, there'd been new rumours that the doorway to the Great Ones (a particularly powerful species of warrior dragons) was out here in this part of Qualterra, so several scout teams had spent a long time looking around, hoping to find some evidence. Most of the Great Ones had been sealed away elsewhere, but a few of the oldest had been helping to move some of the younger dragon species when the portals to their natural world were closed. If the rumours were true, the remaining Great Ones had finished relocating all the dragons they could then came to this world to develop new strategies and hone their skills with the immortal Shrogan. After that, they'd apparently found an ancient site that led to a netherworld—a bubble between worlds created by magix itself—and had gone there, where the Huntowra couldn't detect them, to finish making their preparations for the coming war.

If they could find this entrance, they could hopefully find them, and convince them that now was the time to fight together.

Bryant, one of Peter's older brothers, was supposed to be on this scouting trip, but new refugees had shown up back at the camp, and he was the most qualified to process them. So Jeff had asked Peter to come, trying to find hidden dragons in this godforsaken place. Some of these ravines were familiar to Peter... Could this be the area where he'd come through as a child?

Every time he was made to come here, Peter looked for her too. God, even thinking her name hurt.

Lilah.

What had happened to her in those last moments?

She must've been terrified.

Pain banded Peter's ribs, squeezing until he could barely breathe. He hoped she would pop out of thin air at his side... Despite what the Huntowra had said, he still prayed she was somehow alive. Peter didn't date—it felt too much like cheating on her. He pined for her still, and he would always look for her, no matter what. It hurt too much not to. These brief field trips were really affecting him.

No dragons.

No Lilah.

Not even Mirren, the sword Peter had lost the day he was rescued. Life was shit sometimes.

After a few hours, they reached their destination, a particularly dead-looking part of Qualterra, and made camp for the night.

It was never easy camping in this hellish dump—the

Refugees

constant screeching, the never-ending horde of creatures, and when a storm was brewing...ugh, awful didn't even begin to cover it. They put up specially designed magical barriers to ward off beasts, silence any noise they made, and hide their magix. Then Jeff made a campfire—admittedly, both of them liked that so it was a plus—and they settled in for the night.

Whenever a Talgra scout team came here, they slept sitting up, a natural ability. In truth, Talgra didn't even need a fire as they don't get cold, but it was nice, and today both Peter and Jeff needed to relax.

Jeff was just sitting quietly, watching from the corner of his eye while pretending to look at the newly darkened sky through the barrier roof. Peter had a tonne of respect for his older brother. He was happy it was Jeff here with him and not one of their more annoying brothers. Peter had a destiny he didn't particularly want, and—today more than other days—he wished he'd been born different, more like his brothers.

He missed his sword, Mirren, as well. It'd been a constant companion and, as with all other warriors, Peter felt alone and weak without his sword. Of course, there was his namesake, the dragon who'd befriended Peter when the precious one was born, and now mentored him. The friendship had grown so close that he was almost like an uncle, except that he was a different species. And ate livestock. And didn't like to bathe. Ever.

As the morning broke, several close groups of Shrogan began to stir, and Peter looked over and saw a small cave, with a tiny stream running straight through it... His breath stopped. He couldn't help staring and when he tried to speak, it came out like a grunt crossed with a gargle.

Jeff swung around, ready to battle, but he stood down

when he saw what his brother was looking at. "You want to check it out, brother?" he asked, tension an undercurrent in his careful words.

Peter couldn't speak so just nodded at him stupidly. Emotions welled inside his chest, but it wouldn't do to start bawling like a babe right here, so he took several deep breaths before moving even a fraction. Something about this place tore him apart inside.

They made their way carefully into the dark and damp cave, skirting the remnants of a fire-pit and the bones of small animals. Some skins made a crude nest of sorts in the back corner, and cave paintings adorned the walls as far as the eye could see. It was as though whoever had stayed here had left only moments ago, and Peter half-turned, worried they may come back at any moment. But nobody was here. Nobody had been here for quite some time.

Jeff was scanning the contents of the cave, frowning. "Where do you think your sword went, brother?"

Peter reached out to search for Mirren's aura, but there wasn't as much as residue. "I don't understand. I feel nothing here. Whoever took him did so a long time ago." Anger blazed through him.

I want my sword back. It was a swift thought, gone in an instant.

They took a long time, making sure to process everything, taking pictures and videos with cameras the humans had given them then packing up everything they could to take back to A.S.U. They would need to show all this to the council elders. It was proof of Peter's story from his childhood.

When everything was documented and packed up, Peter

Refugees

took another long look around the cold and desolate space. He shivered. How had he survived here as a tiny child? Even though he'd spent so long looking for this place, he couldn't wait to leave, and Jeff, perhaps sensing this, motioned for them to move out.

After a few sweeps of the immediate area, they started back towards the designated safe area, when Peter saw what looked like a staircase in the mountainside. Odd. Nobody had noticed it before. Jeff was equally surprised when Peter pointed it out. Still, they needed to get back to the council. They would mark the area and let a fresh scouting party explore the stairs.

After taking some pictures and video, Peter carried everything so Jeff could open the portal back to the world with no magix. The council would be delighted.

Chapter 5

As soon as they returned to Earth, Jeff felt the change in atmosphere. As Peter tried to collect himself, Jeff remained quiet and focused on these changes. As an empathic magix being, overwhelming emotions sometimes crippled him, but today was full of energy and hope. The camp was buzzing with excitement, and all the new arrivals had been processed and were settling into their temporary homes. It seemed this bunch had brought hope with them. Or perhaps it was just because Jeff was excited for the first time in a long time.

They'd found the cave Peter had stayed in, and it was exactly as he'd described it. Since then, he'd been all over the place, emotionally. Sad, but also somehow happy. Confused.

"Peter," Jeff said softly, not wanting to upset him further. "I just want you to know that... Well, it's just... Dammit. If you need anything, just let me know, kid. Okay?"

He sort of smiled and mumbled something about not being a pup anymore.

Jeff let it drop. Peter had always been a little delicate, and the youngest of the family, apart from his twin, Ethan, so he would always be a pup in Jeff's eyes. But their older brothers were going to give him a hard time—they always did—so Jeff decided not to. He would simply stand at his side and be there if he was needed. If one or more of their brothers upset Peter too much, Jeff would step in and be the buffer. He was way too

Refugees

raw right now.

* * * *

Three days later, they were getting ready to see the council after having breakfast. Peter had asked his brother not to say anything about what they'd found until the council meeting. The poor guy had been so pale and quiet since the scouting trip that Jeff had thought their mother and father were going to send him to the healers, but he'd made an excuse and they'd let it drop.

Would Emmaline be there? Whenever she saw him, she seemed closed off and distant, and often rushed away with little conversation. Which made him feel stupid for having any desire to see her again...but then, she was the only one who hadn't responded to his charms. Her indifference had annoyed him in the beginning, but she was like that with most males, so he didn't let it upset him anymore. He understood. The problem with Emmaline was...well, she was Emmaline. She'd been this way ever since her cousin was abducted while she watched, helpless. The poor girl must have some horrible memories.

After Lilah was taken, Peter had locked himself away for a week without even eating. He had major temper problems, but he would go off on his own to calm himself. Then, as he got older, he went looking for her—and, of course, accidentally sent himself to Qualterra. One minute they were play-fighting, the next he got this weird look and vanished. He was lucky to survive. Portals at such a young age were very dangerous—the force of the portal and the amount of magix it used generally ripped the being apart, leaving nothing behind. For this reason, the portals were tightly controlled by the council and younglings learned slowly how to create and safely use them.

Nowadays, Emmaline just pottered around with her

flowers, and Peter moped and tried to stay as busy as possible. Today, though, everyone was hopeful and excited. Or maybe it was just him. Either way, they would be in council chambers very soon.

"Hurry up, slowpoke, they aren't going to wait all day," Jeff yelled at Peter.

When he finally got in, he slammed the car door like a pup having a tantrum.

Jeff let out a small chuckle, smiled to himself, and drove. If anyone spoke, Peter might throw up or something. And since cars were one of Jeff's favourite human inventions, he was trying to avoid getting vomit in his.

The drive was all too short and about ten minutes later, they pulled into the car park. Before getting out, they made sure to get everything they would need—which also gave Peter a moment or two before the inevitable endless questioning, and let Jeff gain some control of his excitement.

It was stupid to hope Emmaline was here. She was a busy woman, and she constantly ignored him, for crying out loud. Still, it would sure be nice to see her pretty face, even if only for a moment. Her eyes were the first thing he'd ever noticed about her, like a river of steel, and her hair shone different colours in the light… He breathed in and focused. Today was about what they'd found in the caves of Qualterra.

The council was assembled and seemed bored. Nobody had come with news before, so this would be a shock to them. They gave the two men a cursory glance but kept talking amongst themselves. Jeff and Peter set out all the pictures and items, which must've caught their attention, because they quieted and casually came towards the table, now covered in

Refugees

various pictures and skins.

The grand councilman, a family friend, spoke first, his voice cheerful and affectionate as always. "Well, boys, what have you bought us today, hmm?" He clapped his hands in delight.

Jeff looked over at his brother, but he looked like he was in a coma. "We found the cave Peter spoke of as a child, Samuel."

This was met with a profound silence. They looked between Peter, Jeff, themselves, and the items for some time before the questions began. Peter seemed relieved as he opened up and spoke, outlining what was found and where. After several hours, he was smiling and looking far more relaxed, the tension seemingly leaving his body. The council agreed this was indeed a terrific find, and immediately began planning to investigate the new site as well as the mysterious staircase. They would need several teams so a meeting of all the magix beings was to be held.

Samuel walked them to the door. He quietly spoke out of earshot of the others. "Well done, boys. This is just what we need. There've been other developments, but I can't go into it too much right now. What I will say is that we've heard that a handful of Aggaron survivors may have been sighted only a few months ago." He had a rapt look on his face, and without another word, he hurried off, leaving the brothers standing there, dumbfounded.

Aggaron survivors? That was incredible news if true.

Chapter 6

Four days after the council meeting, Peter and his family were gathering to have dinner. Their mother was making a lasagne—her favourite food—along with several other dishes, while their dad marinated and cooked the steaks and seafood. Ethan was setting up the tables and chairs so everyone could eat outside. There were too many of them to squish into the dining room, especially since they were all adults now. Fifteen fully grown adults in one compact room…not a very pleasant thought.

Jeff was phoning everyone to make sure they were all coming tonight, and he'd told Peter he was bringing enough beer for everyone. He'd been quiet but also sort of hyper today. It must be hard being empathic. Peter personally thought he was getting soft but didn't tease him about it because Jeff had always been there for him.

When Jeff walked into Peter's room to ask him something, he caught Peter staring off into space like an idiot. Again. Peter didn't care; he had high spirits, and for today, at least, he'd celebrate with his family. They needed a carefree moment amongst the turmoil and awful tragedy they'd all endured since the war began. And it had begun with Lilah being taken.

A Huntowra one of the teams captured had laughed cruelly when questioned about Lilah, and told them gleefully how she'd suffered. His *brothers*, as he'd called them, had dropped her from a great height into a horde of Shrogan, not

Refugees

even bothering to watch her be ripped apart. She'd been nothing but a piece of meat to them, thrown away like rubbish. They would pay for that.

As always when thinking of these things, anger burned through him, but he quickly reined in the emotions. They would all have at least this moment of joy. Grandpa had always said it was important to cherish what they had, because, in a flash, it could all be taken away. The precious one, friends and neighbours, the whole world... They had all suffered greatly.

He would be a leader one day. But for now, he was just a man with a lifetime of hurt and a heart that somehow still hoped. Maybe in fifty years, or a hundred, he'd find the strength to love again. It was almost unheard of amongst the Talgra. Nearly everyone had one love and that was it. Since coming to Earth, Peter had studied the cultures and discovered that humans often fell in love with more than one person in their lifetimes. It was rare for them to attach to one being forever as other species did. It had seemed bizarre at first, but now he found it comforting. It gave him hope for his own future.

This had started with a desire to recover Lilah, but now it was so much more. Now it was a war, and a chance to let all families the chance give their loved ones a traditional burial, and so the lost princess could be properly mourned. And there were other things that needed doing. For a start, they needed to re-establish their bases then gather all those willing and able to fight the Huntowra plague.

This sounded relatively easy, but in fact, it was challenging. The battles that had destroyed the alliance and scattered beings to multiple worlds across the universe had left deep scars in the minds of the survivors. Most wanted only to hide away and hope that someone would save them, so convincing them to join this war was proving difficult. Then there were the warriors who'd battled and lost. Even though they were very able, they felt shame and thought they'd be a hindrance, so it was taking a long time to get them to agree to help once more.

The humans of Earth had been surprisingly more accommodating. Even though they had no magix, they were accomplished in many other areas. Where other species relied on magix for everything from building to cooking to fighting, they used tools they'd created and designed. They were creative and could think on their feet to adapt to new situations. Peter had been negotiating with them from the beginning and had formed friendships with a few. It was pleasantly surprising because everyone had thought of humans as a barbaric and unintelligent species. Because of this assumption, there had been problems trying to communicate. When they felt as though they were being treated as less, they responded with hostility and suspicion. That was a mistake. The Talgra had learned more from humans in one year than from centuries of their own cultures, and to humans, aliens were the lesser beings. A species to be studied and pitied.

Peter was always humbled by the humans. Their fleeting lives were all but a breath in comparison to his own, yet they lived more fully and passionately than any other being he'd encountered. Sometimes, he felt on edge, as if he'd missed something important here, something vital. It was impossible to shake the feeling, but he let it go for now. This was stuff he could work through later. For now, they would celebrate.

Peter threw himself into dinner with more excitement than he'd felt since this all began. The Talgra didn't always share meals. Only special occasions and celebrations really

Refugees

prompted families to eat together. But in this place, it was a daily thing. Everyone ate with their loved ones. Did the humans know how special that was? Sitting there and experiencing the atmosphere made Peter feel comfortable for the first time in years.

As they ate, drank and chatted loudly, their mother sang, beautifully. When Dad joined in, though, they all had to cover their ears and lie about his talent. Peter's older brothers play-fought and wrestled each other…which annoyed the hell out of him. He could fight better, and was more powerful, than most warriors but hid his abilities. That was part of his secret. He glanced round at his brothers, thankful they didn't know.

Jeff seemed a little down. He'd wanted to invite Emmaline to this gathering, but she'd snuck off again. Peter often wanted to speak to her about Lilah, but she acted kind of scary. Nobody else seemed aware of it, but he had sensed immense power coming from her. It seemed she was hiding it, as he was, but what power could she possibly have that required her to hide it? Was that why she was always running off?

Jeff loved her, even though he didn't see it yet. He always looked for her, and whenever she was near him, he was calmer. Jeff had quite a reputation with the ladies—almost as though he had some hidden abilities that drew women to him—but all he saw was Emmaline. Would he ever realise how in love with her he was? She sure seemed too busy to notice him, or anyone else, for that matter. Poor Jeff. He would have to step up and place himself in her way if he wanted to attach to her. Peter hoped he would. Everyone deserved to be loved, to be happy, but no one more than Jeff. He'd stood quietly at Peter's side all these years, even when their own family thought Peter was mad and ridiculed him for it. He never stopped believing in his brother, and right now Peter wished he could help him get closer to Emmaline.

As usual, he didn't tell anyone his thoughts. He didn't want to be known as the crazy one again, not now. For the first time in as long as he could remember, he was relaxed and genuinely happy. He wouldn't let that slip away. In this moment, he was just a carefree guy hanging out with his family.

Let the world fall apart. He would fix it tomorrow.

Refugees

Chapter 7

Peter didn't know how any species survived without coffee. There was a coffee shop near council headquarters, and he made a visit to it part of a daily ritual. Across the road, a new bookstore was about to open, and he felt oddly drawn to it, often staring blankly in its direction while sipping his coffee. He'd seen the shadows of someone moving inside and wanted to offer his help but never did. It seemed silly to spend time on such a trivial thing when the galaxy was in danger. Still, there was no denying that he felt connected to the place, without the smallest idea why... He pushed the thought from his mind when Jeff walked into the coffee shop, with Damian trailing him. He frowned slightly. They must've followed him.

They went straight to the counter to order then slowly made their way over to where Peter sat, not saying a word to one another. Something was wrong. They were too quiet. Usually everyone struggled to block out their chatter, but today they weren't speaking at all.

"Hey, guys, what's going on with you two today?" Peter asked.

Damian and Jeff looked at each other then sat, still not saying a word. Crap... Must be really bad news. Damian took a deep breath. "The last scout team in Qualterra found a portal rip going to a world we'd previously thought had none. We've been ordered to put a temporary hold on all searches, including the ones for Lilah." He couldn't even look Peter in the eye when he said it.

Peter pinched the bridge of his nose between his thumb and forefinger, and closed his eyes, taking some deep breaths. Portal rips were dangerous and had to be dealt with to keep the inhabitants of the world from accidentally getting sucked into another world. Or worse.

He let out a frustrated sigh and mumbled, with his hand still covering his face, "That's okay, Damian. I understand this must be the last job you ever wanted to do. I appreciate that you and Jeff came to me personally." And although his heart hurt, he would never let his personal feelings stop something this important.

"Peter, I'm so sorry…but maybe this could be a fresh lead." Jeff fidgeted with his black coffee. "Her remains haven't been found in Qualterra, although the Huntowra told us roughly where she'd been thrown. It's unlikely, but maybe a rip opened under her and she landed somewhere else instead. She had more magix than all of us, after all. And all we know for sure is that she went somewhere, right?"

He had a point. Her remains couldn't have just vanished, and the Shrogan didn't move deceased beings. It seemed they felt that doing so was somehow an unpleasant thing, though nobody understood why. Whatever had happened to her remains, she wasn't where the Huntowra had said she was.

But putting all that aside, they really needed to stabilise the area of the rip for the safety of the beings that inhabited this other world. "So, what new world are we visiting now, guys?" he asked with fake enthusiasm.

They both winced, clearly seeing through Peter's attempt to sound casual, and Damian gritted his teeth before

Refugees

taking a mouthful of his cinnamon and ginger tea. "We aren't going to a new world," he said carefully.

"I don't get it. We need to go there and look around."

"No, Peter, you don't understand. The world the rip opened into is this one. Earth. There are indications that non-human species that sound like the beasts of Qualterra have been coming here for many years now. If that's the case, there's a slight chance she may have somehow ended up here too. Not that I think she did, but if it helps the search while technically not searching for her then, hey...I'm all for it." Damian looked as if he were waiting for something.

Peter was speechless. His human friend had just given them what they so desperately needed: an excuse to keep looking for Lilah. "So, she could have come through here? Your species keeps terrific records of the dead, so are you saying we should search your databases?" Now Peter was getting anxious and a bit upset, but his resolve was firming. They would search here. No matter how slim the possibility, he had to be sure.

"Look, brother, we know it's unlikely. She probably didn't come here. But if she did, well, we all changed physically here. Our stripes are less noticeable, the Vespers' skin looks more human, and there are many other more subtle changes too. It's possible. The humans may have thought her one of theirs, in theory." He seemed on edge and by the sound of it, this conversation was beginning to annoy him. He didn't think she was here. He just wanted to soothe his brother.

"That's right. So we'll search for females who are about the right age and start narrowing it down," Damian added quickly.

Neither of them really believed they would find

anything, but now they had a legitimate reason to search: if she'd come through here, it would prove the rip had been active for some time.

Peter took a deep and steadying breath. "I'll officially put the search for her on hold until I speak to Matthew and we deal with the rip. That's the most urgent situation here. And then, if there's a chance of her being here, her father will need to use his new position as the emperor to help us persuade the others on the council. But the important thing is that we've opened up a new possibility for looking for her." He gulped coffee to cover his sudden emotion and nearly choked on it.

As Peter wiped his watering eyes, he absently looked over at the little bookstore again, just as a tiny young woman walked out. She had waist-length hair, straight as an arrow and pale pink. Her white blouse had ruffles on it and her tight pencil skirt matched her hair. She wore the craziest high heels. How did women walk in those things? Her eyes were a chocolate colour that seemed to clash with her skin. She was pale, and very thin, like she was sickly or something. Peter blinked and frowned.

Damian looked at the woman and then at his friend. After a resigned look, he sighed and got up with a groan. "I'll be right back, guys," he said with a hint of apprehension.

How odd. It wasn't like Damian to be anxious. Peter looked at Jeff, who was frowning after him, apparently sensing that something was off as well. Before they could figure out what he was doing, Damian walked right up to the woman and hugged her tightly. They smiled affectionately and talked for a bit then turned and walked in the direction of the coffee shop.

Crap… He hadn't been looking at her like that. Sure, she was cute, but he wasn't interested in dating her. That was too painful. His brow furrowed, and he rubbed at it, trying to smooth it out without looking like he was doing anything at all. Jeff quietly snickered as the door opened then Peter heard her speaking to Damian. For some reason, his temper flared.

"Okay, sorry to do this, but, guys, this is my little sister Jayne," Damian said a little sheepishly. He held her hand, which was impossibly dainty and pale.

Jayne laughed and elbowed her brother in the ribs, and something about her presence here with Damian was making Peter feel angry, or frustrated, or…something. "Hi, it's really nice to meet friends of my brother. He rarely introduces me. I'm opening the new bookstore across the street." She gestured over her shoulder absently with one hand.

Jeff took her offered hand when she held it out and shook it carefully, clearly also finding her breakable.

If Peter shook her hand, he would probably rip her arm right off. She was so, so tiny. She needed to be bubble wrapped or something. How did she not get seriously hurt? So he just gave a stupid half wave and nodded curtly.

Damian's aura suddenly turned fierce and powerful, and he glared at Peter, radiating fury. That couldn't be helped—he wouldn't risk talking to her and losing his temper with her for no apparent reason—but the change in him made Peter feel ashamed of his behaviour. He'd try to be more polite, even though his emotions still raged. Why was he so angry all of a sudden, or was that even what he was feeling? It seemed a little different from anger, somehow, but he couldn't pinpoint its source.

Sudden silence interrupted his brooding and he started when he realised everyone was watching him. Damian had spoken to him. "Sorry, Damian, what were you saying? I got a little distracted," Peter said, his face growing hotter as he carefully avoided Jayne's eyes. There was something off about her.

"I was just saying that my sister's an expert in obscure and ancient languages. It's a hobby of hers. Perhaps she could help with the translations you seem so obsessed with. That's why you keep coming here, right? To get more books to decode the scribbles or whatever." He looked pointedly at him and waited for an answer.

Peter considered his words very carefully. Working with this tiny woman wouldn't be a good idea, but there was no reason to decline. If he were being honest, they could use a new opinion, but did it have to be hers? "Um, sure. I mean, if you're not too busy, I actually could use some help. If you'd like to, that is." How could one person make him feel so insignificant? It was difficult to speak to her directly, and looking at her made him very uncomfortable. He even had a weird twitch, like someone was grabbing his limbs and jerking them or something. But he forced himself to look at her. She seemed just as wary, and he was relieved for a moment before his temper flared again. Obviously, this would be a tough conversation for them both.

She hesitated, staring at her hands folded in front of her as though they offered some insight. After taking measured breaths, she guardedly raised her eyes. For an instant, the entire universe dropped away. She tore her gaze from Peter, blinking rapidly, and he knew she'd felt the same thing. She, like him, was rocked to the core. What the hell had happened?

When she spoke, Peter wasn't really surprised to find that her voice gave him a shiver. "Erm, well, I won't be able to

Refugees

help very much until after the opening of the bookshop, but I have a few books with my own translations. There are multiple languages. You can see if any look similar. I can bring them to you, if you'd like." She didn't look up from her hands again. In fact, it seemed like she wanted nothing more than to run away and hide.

Great. He actually felt smaller than before. Had he frightened her? And did he actually care if he had? Today was turning out to be the strangest day. "That'd be great. What languages do you know? I haven't looked at many Earth languages yet." Surprisingly, he was interested. He'd only asked because he wanted to be polite for Damian's sake, but now he was curious. And it seemed Damian picked up on this, softening a little towards him. Peter also silently noted that she hadn't reacted to his comment about Earth languages, so Damian must've told her about them.

She fidgeted with her wrist absently, as if there were something there, but both her arms were bare, though there seemed to be a faint shimmer to her skin. She was so nervous. Were all the women of Earth like that? He hadn't really taken any notice before now. "I actually speak nearly twenty distinct languages fluently. Most are dead or obscure though. It just seems easy for me to learn them, and even easier to speak them. My favourite would have to be Sumerian. Do you have a favourite?"

Wow. Twenty languages? That was impressive. She seemed less shy talking about languages. "Mm, I don't think I've considered if any are my favourites. And I haven't heard of Sumerian, but it sounds interesting. When could you bring me those translations?" Peter relaxed a bit as they talked, but he was still very wary of her.

Damian interrupted them just as she was about to answer, and Peter's anger flared again. "Oh shoot, I nearly forgot," he said, getting up and stretching, "we'd better make a move. Mom will have kittens if we're late for dinner again."

Jayne smiled ruefully and got up. Then she turned, and her eyes met Peter's for a second time. It was like being blown apart and made deaf, numb, and hyperaware all at the same time…and he wanted to feel that way. Just as he looked away, she caught her breath, obviously just as affected. This was bad. Something here was really off. Peter bit down on his lip without thinking as they left the coffee shop, drawing blood. Jeff stared at his brother, clearly feeling his turmoil. Peter didn't know what to say so he just watched Damian and his sister cross to the bookstore, and for a second, it felt like a piece of him had been ripped away. She turned at the door of the shop and clutched her chest, as though struggling to breathe, then gave a small nod and a wave and went inside.

Jeff and Peter sat in silence and finished their coffee. Of course he would know his brother was shaken up. When Peter got up and moved to leave, Jeff was right beside him. Peter didn't particularly want his brother, or anyone, to give him a hard time for walking when it was simple enough to teleport—one of the few abilities they could use here—but it seemed he wasn't going to. He just walked at his brother's side and said nothing.

Chapter 8

What had been up with Peter today? The Talgra rarely let their emotions get to them, so his rudeness earlier was infuriating. Damian had always had a terrible temper and was protective of his little sister—she'd been through more than most and was actually quite shy—but when he'd seen Peter looking at her, he'd figured she might like to meet him. Beings from other places were kind of an obsession for her, and she needed all the distractions she could get from her illness.

She was getting sicker by the day, and the doctors had no idea what was wrong with her. At first, they'd diagnosed asthma then some sort of lung disease but now they said that her illness was completely mysterious. One thing was for sure: if they couldn't find a cure soon, she would die. It was like her body was being squashed by an invisible force, and it was so bad now that she often feinted from lack of oxygen. If she could help distract Peter and decode this prophecy, that would be a win-win in Damian's book. That was why he'd given her the money to open this little bookstore. He didn't know how long she had, but he would give her everything he could to keep her occupied and happy for as long as possible.

Their mother was constantly stressing out over Jayne being so determined to lead a normal life, but her worry just made Jayne dig her heels in. Damian had tried to convince her to take it slowly, but she insisted on doing everything she could for as long as she could. She'd been quiet after meeting Jeff and

Peter, and he wondered why. He'd been sure she would ask a gazillion questions about them and their culture, but she didn't say anything and she had a look of utter sadness on her face. He was about to ask her about it when she finally looked up and grinned from ear to ear.

Uh-oh.

That meant trouble. She was scheming something. His worry vanished, instantly replaced with a sort of fear.

"Damn, what's going on in your head, Kitty?" Kitty was a nickname he'd given her due to her many cat-like qualities.

"Nuffin," she said with a pout and a look of total innocence that fooled nobody. Only Jayne could look like a grown up but act like a child...and still seem completely elegant.

Definitely up to something. He gave her a big-brother look and decided he'd get it out of her later, with their mother's help.

Ashlyn was a beautiful woman, but she'd never remarried after the death of her husband. She'd adopted Damian and then, a few years later, Jayne, as though living alone had been too painful for her. She was a secretive woman who was fiercely protective and never spoke of her past. It seemed as if her life had begun when he was eight years old, and oddly enough, he couldn't remember anything from before then either. His councillor had said it was perhaps from the trauma of seeing his birth mother die, and he'd always accepted this, but sometimes he wondered if there was something he should've been remembering.

He had no one to ask, because—even though his biological mother had been her best friend—Mom had never

Refugees

allowed it. The sum total of his knowledge about his mother's life was that she'd died in Ashlyn's arms, begging her to hide Damian and protect him, and that he'd had a younger sister who died when she was five. He didn't even remember the name he'd been born with, or who his father was.

All the boys at school had gone on camping and fishing trips with their fathers, but he hadn't had anybody like that, so he'd simply pretended to be sick so he could stay home. Bothering his mother with that kind of thing while she struggled to look after a seriously ill child wasn't an option, so he'd pushed the feelings of hurt, and loneliness, and emptiness aside. He'd put on a brave face, not even telling his mates his life story, in case they pitied him. Now *he* was the man in his family, taking care of his mom and his sister.

Jayne had always looked up to him. They'd been close right from the beginning, as if they'd always known each other, even though he'd been ten when she came to them. They even looked somewhat alike, and he had dreams sometimes that she was his proper sister, but his therapist explained that it was just because she was the same age as his biological sister and he desired the blood connection. To have someone the same as he was…it was a powerful wish.

Jayne was fluttering about the store now, putting stock up on shelves and cases. She seemed so relaxed doing this kind of thing, and it made him feel better to just sit quietly and watch her. She was the single most graceful person he knew, and she never got flustered. He felt a wave of sadness that she was suffering; she would never let on, but he knew she was in pain. Sometimes, it hurt her so bad she looked like she was having a heart attack, and other times she seemed to go vacant then grab at her left arm and scream like she was on fire. The doctors had no answers. They waffled on that her nerves were likely affected by the constant lack of oxygen...but even they didn't know why her left arm was affected the worst. Life sucked sometimes.

He pondered both Jayne and Peter's behaviour earlier. If he hadn't known any better, he'd have thought there was chemistry there, but the Talgra didn't have multiple loves and Peter's love had attached to him from birth. It seemed strange to Damian, but Jeff had explained that when children attached, they didn't feel love the same way as adults. They were like best friends who grew into a more mature type of love, and they stayed together for their whole existence. But something had happened today. There was an electricity between them that had physically affected both him and Jeff. Did the Talgra ever feel lust? He would ask Jeff when he saw him next.

* * * *

Jayne loved that her brother stayed quietly at her side. He was her rock when things got too much for her to bear, and she was still shaken by meeting Peter. There'd been an instant connection between them, and it had been all she could do not to touch him. She'd wanted to throw herself into his arms and cocoon herself there, embraced by the smell of him, the sound of his voice and the beat of his heart. As though that would fix all the wrongs in her world. As though she somehow belonged there, belonged to him.

But that was nonsense. She was a grown woman, and these fantasies had no practical use. She'd been sick for as long as she could remember. That was the only reason she'd indulged in these strange urges. She'd needed a distraction, and he'd provided it. Except...those brief moments with him were the first time she'd ever felt relief from her constant and

Refugees

unbearable pain, and she'd finally been able to breathe. But the second she'd walked across the road, all the air left her lungs with a whoosh. She had no idea what had happened or why, but she did know two things. One: she wanted to see him again, and not just because of the strange relief he seemed to provide. Two: she felt a powerful and irresistible connection to him that both frightened and excited her.

She'd often imagined meeting some tall, dark, and handsome man, who magically made her whole life better, but this was no dream. When their eyes had connected for the briefest moment, the world had tilted and slipped away. She saw again the familiar images of a world unlike any she knew, with a crystal-tipped castle smothered in stunning flowers that shone in the night, surrounded by a quaint little village with cobbled-stone streets. A massive city was just visible in the distance, and the castle itself was so big it had to have been miles wide. A planet that was almost pink hung in the sky, surrounded by golden rings and a purple-tinged moon. There were two other moons, small and off white, on the opposite side of the sky.

A powerful king stood in a massive green circle surrounded by golden symbols at the centre of an enormous stone square. A symbol hung above the king's crown, so bright she could barely see it, though it might've been wings. His hair was streaked with white as though he wore ice in it, his clothes were leather, and his heavy black cape seemed almost liquid. A gold sword dangled from his left hand, covered in markings and attached to his left arm by a crisscrossing of fine gold chains. He had several gold bands on his upper arms and some kind of tribal markings where his skin showed. He stood casually but seemed tense, as though waiting for something, and he wore a slight scowl. Even though she didn't recognise him, she felt drawn to him by a force as inescapable as gravity, and his pain called out to her.

She'd had the dream many times—and each time she'd wake up crying, her heart breaking for the king—but this was the first time she'd had it while awake. Somehow, something connected it to Peter. She'd found him slightly annoying, and he'd seemed bored by her presence, even a little angry, though she had no idea why. She would tell her mother.

The first time she'd had a vision, it had scared her silly, and her mother had helped her to accept the gift. She'd had her close friend Mrs Whitley make up a herbal remedy for Jayne's anxiety, which had really helped—for most of the visions. Sometimes, though, she vanished to another place in her dreams, and nothing helped. She would be asleep and then she would suddenly be standing in a strange place in a crowd of people. She could never see the faces of these people, whoever they were, and they were all making weird humming sounds, like a loud buzzing over talking. It was painful and overwhelming, and when she woke up screaming in her bed, her left arm would be bright red and swollen like she'd burnt it. Nobody knew why, though, or how to stop it, so she had to just live with it.

She had a strange scar on the inside of her left wrist— an incomplete oval that could've been a silhouette of something except that it was slightly twisted off to the side, as if stamped crookedly. There were a few little gathered spots on it as well, as though there was more to the scar. Jayne actually quite liked it, but when she thought about it, her heart hurt, a powerful wave of nausea rolled through her, and she felt like she was missing something very special to her. Her therapist suggested the scar was some kind of birthmark and possibly reminded her

Refugees

of her past family, even though she had no memories of them at all, only of monsters and pain.

She'd always assumed this was the horror of her accident, which had ended up with her on life support in a hospital. No family had come forward, and she hadn't matched any of the profiles of missing children. According to her medical team, she'd been electrocuted and possibly run over, shattering all her bones. Based on her injuries, it seemed there'd been a deliberate attempt on her life, but by whom? Had someone taken her against her family's will? Was anyone looking for her? But then why wasn't she on the missing children database?

She'd thrown herself into study, and later, work. She hated stillness, and not learning every day made her feel as though she would shrivel up and die. Learning other languages and about other cultures seemed a natural thing to do, but she had no idea why. She just needed to know as much as she could about as many cultures as possible. It was life or death to her. She used to imagine herself saving the world with her knowledge, like David Levinson in *Independence Day*, but now that she was older, the knowledge was simply a distraction from the pain of her treatments and her worries about her mother and brother.

Damian was her best friend, and the best brother anyone could ever have, and her mom loved her even when she had learnt how sick her daughter was, she'd chosen to keep her and make sure Jayne had every ounce of love she could give. Her friends were amazing as well. They often gifted her with wigs and silly shoes so she could dress up and be someone else each day. It let her forget about her pain and exhaustion and have fun with her life.

And now she'd finally met a being from another world. Although she hadn't ever imagined feeling so shy and uncertain when the time finally came. Why did she react to him the way she had? She almost felt like she knew him from somewhere. Which was, of course, impossible.

She needed to get near Peter again. He was such an intriguing being to her already, and she'd only just met him. Helping him would be a brilliant way to learn more about him. And if he was rude to her, she would simply pretend it didn't bother her. He could get over whatever made him such a grump.

She hummed a cheery tune while she finished up for the day. While she worked, her brother looked around the store, seemingly distracted—but she knew better. He wanted answers from her. And he was probably still brooding about Peter's reaction to her. Apparently, it wasn't normal for him to behave that way, and Damian was very upset by it. He was so protective of her that she almost felt sorry for Peter, but she knew better than to say anything.

She let out a sigh and turned off the lights, knowing her brother would follow her out of the shop.

Chapter 9

Friday was family dinner night—a tradition Ashlyn had started when she adopted her children. It had changed as they grew up, but they still met every week on Friday. Jayne lived with Damian in a roomy four-bedroom house with a swimming pool and all the comforts one could hope for—one of the ways Dae cared for his little sister.

Ashlyn was so grateful for her children. They'd been close from the very beginning, as though they'd always been together. And they'd needed each other so badly when they were little. Damian had amnesia brought on by the trauma of his other mother's passing, and Jayne only saw monsters and felt pain when she tried to remember anything of her life before. The doctors agreed it was likely her brain trying to protect her, though it was possible some mild brain damage had occurred. Ashlyn knew differently, though, in both her children's cases.

She'd often wondered if she should tell them or if they were better off not knowing. What was the point in dragging up the past when it had no place in their futures? But five years ago, everything had changed when the Roswell Greys attacked and the knowledge of life elsewhere was out to the general population. Should she now tell her children what she knew? She very much doubted it would be distressing to them, but she didn't want to burden them with more questions. Or perhaps she was just being selfish…

Her son's car pulled into the driveway.

Jayne didn't drive because of her medical problems, but Damian was always on hand to take her anywhere, and he always dropped everything to make sure she got to where she wanted or needed to go. A good man, who always put his sister first. She hoped whoever he eventually fell in love with would understand that. Would deserve him.

Ashlyn could hear her children now, Damian speaking gruffly and Jayne giggling at him. He was the only one who could ever get her to let down her guard and laugh like that. Despite herself, Ashlyn felt a tinge of jealousy. They were so very close... She took a steadying breath before they reached the side gate.

Jayne rushed to her mother and wrapped her in a tight hug. Ashlyn hugged her back but shot a quick, pointed look at Damian before turning back to her. "Hey, my little kitten. How was your day? You seem extra happy. Is there something I should know about?" She tried not to sound too interested.

"No, Mama, I just had a good day. I even got to meet some of Dae's friends." Jayne hadn't called her Mama for years now. While she was very touched Jayne was in this strangely affectionate mood, it also worried her.

Ashlyn tried to control her voice but a hint of worry slipped out nonetheless. "Well, come on then. Let's sit and have dinner. I've hardly eaten today. Abby was flat out at the herbalist, so I stepped in and helped her out."

Damian was a little quiet tonight, but he seemed in good spirits, so she put the thought aside for now and concentrated on dishing out the casserole. It had been her husband's family recipe, and Damian's favourite, and she refused to change it. As she spooned out the mashed potato and ladled generous amounts of casserole on top, Jayne turned to her brother.

Refugees

"I can't wait to get started on those translations. I wonder if the language Peter's trying to decipher is similar to any of ours." Her whole face lit up, and Damian looked at her with a wry and slightly calculated look, which instantly put Ashlyn on her guard.

She cast a slightly anxious look at her daughter then went back to serving dinner. Something was definitely going on here. Jayne didn't seem to notice her brother's look, though, and she dug into her dinner with enthusiasm, as though she hadn't eaten in weeks. She hadn't had an appetite like this for years. What had happened today?

* * * *

Jayne chatted all through dinner, gorging herself and talking around mouthfuls. "So then I was thinking about all the languages and how some of them seemed to have no proper basis here. Could they have been from another world? I mean, it seems possible, right? Some of our ancient cultures even say they were brought here from the stars and stuff, and it doesn't seem so crazy to think that now. When I see Peter again, I thought I'd ask him about some of the other places he's been to, and maybe he'll want to learn more about Earth too. I could share as much as I can with him." She finished with a sigh.

So that was what she was up to. If she had her way, she would grill him on every aspect and every little detail of all the worlds he knew about…but why? His sister wasn't the scheming sort, but she was determined. He considered warning Peter, but then felt a smug little surge of pleasure. Peter could stew on it for a while. It seemed his sister was going to nonstop grill him, and if she was half this chatty, Peter would soon be sorry he'd been so rude to her.

When the dinner dishes were done, Ashlyn surprised

Jayne with some new outfits she'd been buying here and there, and while Jayne was trying them all on upstairs in her old room, Ashlyn turned to Damian with a suspicious look. "What's happening here, Dae?"

"I honestly have no idea, Ma. She met one of my friends from work, and since then, she's had this bouncy energy. It was so weird. She seemed to breathe better. Her whole face relaxed like she wasn't hurting as much and then when we left, she got all of about fifty feet away from Peter and all the usual stuff came back. You know, clutching her arm, breathless… I think she's planning something, but I don't know what."

Damian was still furious at Peter about his behaviour today. For as long as he could remember, Peter had been the calmest and kindest, the most reasonable, of his brothers. They were all outstanding people, and though Jeff was his favourite, Peter was a close second. If he were being honest, though, if he had to pick a Taylor brother to work a mission with, it would be Ethan, Peter's twin. He had the fastest reflexes, and his brain was like a computer, almost instantly calculating all the possible scenarios then computing the safest course of action to take, making all their jobs a little safer. Jeff's empath-based magix was brilliant for things like interrogations, and nobody could hide from his abilities, so he could track fugitives by their emotional state.

Peter was an unknown. He'd been chosen as a warrior (as had all his brothers except Jye) so he clearly had the potential, but he'd never donned the warrior uniform of his people, and refused to fight in any battles. His brothers said it was because of the little girl who'd bound him to her, but Damian couldn't help thinking there was more to it than that. Wouldn't her loss have made Peter want to fight? Wouldn't he

Refugees

want revenge?

The logical conclusion was that there was another reason he wasn't donning the uniform, but Peter wasn't about to tell. Damian was the only one who seemed to have realised that Peter might've had another reason for his choice, but he kept it to himself. He didn't want to cause a problem for his friend by speaking up.

Instead, Peter spent his days buried in books and scrolls, trying to learn their languages and understand the cryptic meanings of long-forgotten writings. Right now, he was devoting every second of his time trying to decode some bizarre prophecies, which seemed pointless, but if it helped him feel like he was doing something, so be it. Damian tried to think logically about why Peter's reaction to his sister had upset him so much, but it simply made no sense to him at all. He would just have to confront his friend and ask him why he'd been so rude.

Chapter 10

Damian was tired, both he and Jayne were quiet on the ride home. It was nice having her live with him. It was a practical arrangement, and honestly, he enjoyed his sister's company. Jayne had such quirky taste in everything from clothes to shoes and decor. He'd decorated her bedroom to surprise her when he bought his home. He'd built her a roomy closet for all her clothes and outfits, and an accessory room which doubled as a dressing room because she had so many wigs, contact lenses, makeup, and about a tonne of jewellery—some genuine and expensive but most costume jewellery and stuff she'd made herself. There were also a few pieces he'd made for her when they were younger and she'd been in hospital. She point blank refused to get rid of anything he'd made, and carefully repaired the pieces when they broke as though they were the most precious items in the entire world.

He smiled a little wryly at the thought of all her costumes and accessories. How did she make it all seem so normal and fun? Some of her costumes were outrageous. Tonight, their mother had given her about a year's worth of extra clothes. Soon, she would need a whole new closet to store them all in. He wondered idly if he could get her to donate some of her older costumes and accessories to charity then chuckled to himself for even thinking it. Of course she would, but more would find its way to her closets. As he pulled into the garage, he glanced over at her. She looked very relaxed—more than he could ever remember seeing her, in fact. How curious today had been.

Refugees

* * * *

Jayne was daydreaming, looking at nothing in particular, and it took a moment for her to notice her surroundings. They were home, and all she wanted in the world was to put her new clothes away and get showered and into some pyjamas. She was gathering her stuff when Dae came round to help her. They made their way to her room and put all the clothes in her closet on the little love seat she'd restored herself. She would sort them out and put them away after her shower, if she felt up to it.

* * * *

While she picked out some pyjamas and headed for the luxurious bathroom to shower, Damian went down to the kitchen and put the kettle on. He loved nothing more than a hot cocoa with cinnamon to unwind at the end of a huge day. He automatically got two mugs down and spooned cocoa into them. It had become a ritual for the siblings to share an evening cocoa no matter how late it was. If one came home late and the other was asleep, they woke the other one up just for cocoa. He was smiling at his memories and rummaging through the draw when she came into the kitchen and sat at the counter. Her unicorn pyjamas were almost as crazy as her daily outfits, but she'd removed the wig, her makeup, and contact lenses. She'd brushed her long curly hair until it shone and flowed down to her waist. Her eyes were green and sparkling. He much preferred her like this. He took the kettle off the stove as it whistled and poured out the water.

* * * *

Jayne watched quietly from her stool, her leg tucked up under her bottom, and rested her face in her hands. She loved watching Dae like this. He was so at ease. He was always present and she felt so safe with him near. He slowly stirred the hot cocoa and handed her one of the steaming mugs without even looking up.

"Thanks, Dae. For everything today."

"Anytime. So…um…listen, Peter isn't the dating kind of guy," he blurted. "He had someone, but she was murdered. I just thought you should know, okay?"

"I wasn't interested in dating him, Dae, I'm just really curious about him. I feel good today, and besides, it will be fun to go through those translations."

"Just take it easy on him, okay, Kitty?" he replied a little sharply. "He's actually a really friendly guy, and I know you're scheming up something to do with him… I'm just saying to be nice." He let out a gush of breath, which whistled slightly.

Jayne could tell he was cranky and a little defensive, though not at her. She remained quiet and they finished their cocoa in silence.

Refugees

Chapter 11

After washing her mug out and saying goodnight to her brother, she quietly settled in for the night. She began to make a new necklace but fell asleep halfway through—the beads rolled from her hands…and she was somewhere else. The streets were spotless, and the smell of all sorts of foods wafted on the air. A girl was saying something, but the words were muffled, like a television set losing signal, and sounds came from the nearby houses. This place was familiar to her, but she didn't recognize it.

The air changed, like there was static electricity everywhere, and then she saw the monsters. A few paces from her, they were blurred, hard to make out—but she could tell they had deformed features and pointy teeth. They appeared to be happy, and this made her feel a little scared. Nausea churned in her gut, and things shifted again.

This place had no roads, but there were lots of cliffs, and something was screeching. The colours here were wrong, and it smelled like rot. She didn't like this place and tried to wake herself, but she couldn't. After a while listening to the screeches, things shifted again.

The boy was also fuzzy, but his eyes weren't—they were the most incredible blue she'd ever seen. He had stripes, angled as though they were tattoos and perfectly arranged. She suddenly felt as though she knew him, and for a fraction of a second, an image of the royal man popped into her head.

In the next second, the entire world exploded and she was falling through lightning. Just when she thought the lightning was nearly gone, she saw two bright spots, which came ever closer until something solid smashed into her. There was a moment of brief agony then darkness filled with strange words and smells. It seemed to go on forever then she was struggling to breathe, people were screaming, and she was aching all over. When she finally managed to open her eyes, she wished she could go back to the darkness. The brightness hurt, made her feel like she was on fire. She didn't know where she was.

Fear clutched at her, but then a woman with a kind, sad face entered her room. She introduced herself as Loretta and announced she was taking her away.

The memory shifted again. She was playing by herself. The other kids said she was weird and didn't like playing with her because she was so serious all the time. Today, though, she didn't care. Today was a special day; she was told to wear her finest dress because a woman was coming to meet her. She wasn't sure why, though—nobody wanted to adopt her because she was sick. Perhaps this woman knew how to make her better. A dark blue sedan pulled up in the driveway, and a beautiful woman with blond hair climbed out. She was in her late thirties or early forties and had a boy with her.

She made her way casually up the stairs as though she did this every day, and Jayne giggled nervously. Lotti hushed her with a flap of her hand—but was smiling kindly so she wasn't in any real trouble—and went to greet the blond woman and curly-haired boy. They whispered in an unfamiliar, pretty language for a few minutes then Lotti helped the lady take her coat off.

Refugees

The boy was a little older than Jayne, and he looked at her strangely. She felt oddly anxious; she didn't want him to hate her or think she was some sort of freak. He seemed a little cautious himself and kept side-eying her. Slowly, he worked his way over and quietly said hello. She knew right then that he wasn't like the other children, and she felt an immediate closeness to him. Within a few minutes, he had her laughing for the first time she could ever remember. She would never forget the moment; it had been the beginning of her life.

Chapter 12

Jayne woke up feeling very lethargic. Her sleep had been full of memories and nightmares, but despite that, she didn't have any pain so she supposed she was doing well. As she climbed out of bed, she stood on one of her beads. It made a tiny clinking noise as it skidded from under her toe. Sighing, she bent down and retrieved the beads she'd been working with last night before she fell asleep.

She was a little dazed still. She'd gone somewhere else again last night in her sleep, but unlike every other time it had happened, she hadn't woken up screaming or in agony—and although she was confused, she wasn't scared anymore. She took her time, getting up with slow and deliberate movements, expecting the crushing pain she always felt—but it didn't come.

Jayne rifled through her cupboard, and eventually settled on a pale blue 50s dress with white frills on the hem and collar and paired it with knee-high lace-up boots that were almost the same colour. She added a silver chain belt with suns and flowers and chose violet contact lenses to give a quirky contrast to her look. As she was adjusting her silver wig, her phone started buzzing. She didn't really feel up to speaking right now, and almost let it go to voicemail. In the end, though, she answered the call as she headed downstairs.

It was her book supplier calling with grim news. Her shipments were all delayed for at least a week, meaning she had nothing to do for the entire week. Although…maybe she could

Refugees

use this week off to learn more about Dae's friend and begin the translations.

Her mind wandered as she went into the kitchen to try to figure out what she wanted for breakfast. As it turned out, she didn't need to worry about that as Dae had gotten up early and was busy making scrambled eggs with toast, tomatoes, and hash browns. He was humming loudly and jumped as she entered the room, clearly lost in his own little world. Jayne set the table while Dae finished cooking. As they started eating, Dae looked up and smiled quickly to his sister then went back to humming. Huh. Dae was always chatty over breakfast. She chewed her mouthful of egg slowly while staring at her brother.

"Dae," she said tentatively.

"Hmm?" He was still distracted with his plate.

"Dae," she repeated louder, and this time he looked right at her. "Are you okay?" She hated prying into her brother's life like this, but it was so out of character for him to be so absentminded.

"I'm fine, Kitty. Why?" He smiled as he poured golden syrup on his eggs instead of Lancashire relish.

She opened her mouth to tell him then shrugged and mumbled, "Just wondering. You seem…a little distracted."

He took a bite then gagged. "Ah, crap. Thanks, brat, you coulda warned me."

Jayne snorted a laugh.

He ran to the sink and washed his mouth out while she finished her own breakfast. He could be so dramatic sometimes.

* * * *

Damian had to drop some new vests at work before he took Jayne to her store. Working for the Alien Species of the Universe (A.S.U) was amazing but also dangerous, so the government had insisted that employees wear full combat gear at all times in case of an attack. Seemed a bit overkill, but it was the law, so he obeyed. The vests had arrived two days ago and been sent to the wrong warehouse, so he'd agreed to pick them up.

Jayne gathered her things and packed it in the backpack she carried all her translations in. She clearly intended to get them to Peter today.

"So, any message for Peter to go with those scribbles?" He wiggled his eyebrows at her. There was no way she would let him give the translations to Peter, but he'd hoped she would at least give him a chance to tell his friend off for his rudeness.

"No way, doofus. I'm delivering these myself. The last shipment of books was delayed by a week. They just phoned and apologised," she said with a little smirk. "That means I can come to work with you all week."

Damian sighed. He didn't mind his sister was coming to work with him. He just hoped she didn't annoy anyone. He'd only suggested she help Peter to keep her occupied, but maybe he shouldn't have said anything. She'd been acting very oddly since yesterday.

* * * *

As they pulled into the parking lot of A.S.U, Jayne again seemed to feel better. How odd. Were her treatments finally starting to work? Could it be that she'd just needed time to let her body react? She hadn't felt this good for as long as she could remember. For the first time in her entire life, she felt like she

Refugees

could breathe without being suffocated. She had no pain, and she seemed hyperaware of everything around her. She could only hope it wasn't temporary.

Jayne took a slow, deep, and steadying breath then unclipped her seatbelt and hauled up her backpack—it was heavy because she'd brought everything with her. She would see if any were close to the language Peter was trying to decipher, and then maybe they could start decoding the mysterious writings. She couldn't wait. She loved languages and had a real knack for them, and the chance to see a new one—one no other earthling had seen... She was so excited she almost let out a bubble of nervous laughter but held it back so she didn't upset her brother.

He was very sensitive right now about his friend and seemed to be wary of her being here. She would find Peter and they would sit quietly and go through the translations. Dae could be a grump elsewhere. She wouldn't bother him.

Chapter 13

Jayne hadn't been here before, so everything was wondrous and new to her. The entrance was a sweeping stone stairway that curled outwards at the base then narrowed towards the top. The heavy doors reminded Jayne of an ancient castle. The solid dark wood and metallic trimmings were very gothic, but it was definitely modern.

Inside, Jayne stopped dead. This place was gigantic and filled with oddities. To the left was a long hallway with doors of different shapes and sizes seemingly strewn haphazardly along the inner wall. The outer wall was completely made up of windows, and every window had a different view. Intricate paintings of strange things and places hung between the ornate doorways. The archway to the right was made of live plants in flower. Vines curled down randomly, and the pastel-blue flowers were the size of side plates. She'd seen no plant like it before, but it reminded her of something. Even the scent, like jasmine crossed with roses, made her feel at home. A solid wooden door seemed almost hidden within the arch of the strange, beautiful plant, and this door was somehow…threatening. The atmosphere felt dark and electric—or she was simply overreacting.

She couldn't shake the desire to explore this place, her curiosity more intense than she could ever remember it being, but she was here for a purpose: to help Peter. And pepper him with questions. There were so many, but surely he would answer them as long as she dedicated enough time to the

Refugees

translations. She would be careful not to get too carried away, though. Perhaps she should write a list and then prioritise what she really wanted to know.

Damian pointed to the oddly creepy door on the right. "Come on. This is the way to the primary meeting area. Try not to wander off, though, okay? This place is like a maze."

"Dae, why is that door hidden?" she asked uncertainly.

He looked at her and smiled with some surprise. "They don't want random strangers wandering about in this area so they added the Starling Trumpets. They're a rare flower from a planet called Meakra. Nobody's actually trying to hide the door, though, but I guess I can see why you would think that. One end of the hall is so open and bright, while this end is earthier and darker. I think that's just a coincidence though." He kept his voice low as they slowly wandered down to the primary meeting area, and Damian only paused briefly to readjust his uniform.

When they reached the archway, Jayne took a deep breath and instantly felt as though she were completely safe and relaxed. Dae let out a chuckle, which he tried to cover with a quick cough.

"What are you laughing at?"

He looked instantly remorseful. "The scent is a powerful relaxant. It helps ease any negativity and acts like a repellent to certain creatures and beings, giving them a colossal headache. They can't stand being near the plant, which is why it grows all around the palace on Meakra—it helped prevent anything too scary from getting close to the royal family. If any dangerous critters were to find their way to this world, this plant would slow them down before they got out into the public. The primary meeting area also has a magix ring and barrier. They use it as a safe point for opening portals to the other worlds, but we wanted an extra precaution in case something went wrong. And this door is the only entrance that isn't sealed with magix barriers. It's better to be safe than sorry, right?" He smiled grimly then gently nudged her back to usher her through the archway and followed her into the strange meeting room.

Jayne let out a gasp. It had Starling Trumpets growing everywhere, in every direction she could see. There was a large intricate green circle at the far end of the room with etchings surrounding the outside. A large ornate rectangle encompassed the ring and the area all around it, like a basketball court. An enormous stairway led from the right side to an upper floor, with the Starling Trumpets draping down them like a living wall. The upper floor was open so she could see the landing and another hall. Spaced throughout the room were other doorways leading away, with the plants delicately swept aside like a curtain. At the far end, a balcony acted as a viewing point of some kind, under an ornate glass ceiling.

On the left side of the room, papers and maps were scattered over high benches, and there was some kind of high-tech 3D map table, with mountains and buildings, rivers that moved, and trees and plants that swayed in the breeze. Beyond these, there were two other doorways and a stone archway in between them, with stairs leading down and an old-fashioned light fixture that could've been from medieval times.

She shivered unconsciously and stepped closer to her brother, who chuckled again. "I forgot this place can be so overwhelming for newbies."

She nodded, though she wasn't exactly overwhelmed, acknowledging that it was impressive and somewhat

Refugees

forbidding.

"So," he clapped his hands, "I want you to wait right here for me while I go let the others know you've arrived." He led her over to a line of benches on the right side of the room near the staircase. "Do me a favour, Kitty, don't go into the rectangle, okay? It won't hurt you, but if anyone opens a portal, the barriers will come up," he gestured at the rectangular outline, "and you'll get stuck in there. Just stay here, and I'll be right back."

"I'll stay right here." She smiled. "Don't get lost."

The corners of his mouth twitched.

Chapter 14

Damian was gone for about five minutes when a man came in through the same door. Maybe a little over six feet, he was muscular but not overly bulky. His chocolate hair was short and spiked, with a hint of curls near his temples, and his eyes were a sparkling grey blue. He walked as though completely at ease here, and it took a minute for him to notice her. When he did, he stiffened and his eyes turned from sparkle to steel instantly.

"Who are you? And how'd you get in here?" He looked around as if trying to find a broken window or something, frowning slightly. Heat rose in her cheeks. "Are you one of the new scouts who were supposed to be here last week? Cause if so, you're kind of late." His voice was hard and loud, but not unkind, and held a touch of petulance.

Jayne sat there and stared, not knowing what to say. Who was he? Did he have the authority to remove her or was he just curious?

She was trying to figure out what to say when he spoke again, pronouncing each word carefully. "Are you deaf?" He signed each word as he spoke. "I can sign. I've been learning for about two years now." He poked himself in the chest with his thumb, obviously proud of his achievement.

Anger flashed through her, but it faded almost instantly as a powerful calm snuffed it out—the Starling Trumpets' work. It was a little annoying that she couldn't be angry when

Refugees

she wanted to be, and it only added to her confusion.

Damian came back, and Peter was with him.

Peter eyed the man with a slightly sour look and grimaced then sighed. "Dammit, Bryce, you were supposed to be here three hours ago," he snapped, but there was no real bitterness in his tone—clearly, he'd expected the man's behaviour.

"Well, I was busy," replied Bryce childishly. "Besides, with your inflated head in that meeting there wouldn't have been enough room for my gorgeous self." He smirked and rolled his eyes.

Surprisingly, this made Peter laugh, and an odd zinging sensation started in her lower spine then went all the way up to her brain, where it gave her pins and needles all around her head. She took a deep, steadying breath, intensely aware that the tightness in her chest had disappeared again. Odd, but nice. A shiver went through her and she stood up quickly, her excitement back.

Peter flicked a quick glance in her direction then went back to talking with Bryce, Damian joining in. Jayne hesitated then went and stood nearer the group, who were now chatting animatedly, teasing each other, and play-fighting. After a few minutes, Dae gestured to his sister to come closer. She walked straight to him and hugged his waist, needing the comfort.

Bryce turned to Damian with an openly curious expression, his eyes fixed on Jayne's arm around his waist. He winked at her but spoke to Damian. "I didn't realise you were popular with the ladies. Figured you were a monk, but now I see you've been hiding this beauty. That's cold, bro. You coulda at least introduced us to your girlfriend sooner. Or are you scared she'll like me better?" he added teasingly.

Peter snapped, "For crying out loud, Bryce, give it a rest already," and his voice held genuine anger.

Bryce blinked in shock, and Dae stiffened. Both men looked at him in genuine surprise.

"She's his sister, you idiot," he added tersely, and Jayne giggled then flushed.

He gave her a tiny side glance and the corners of his mouth twitched, but if she hadn't been looking directly at him, she wouldn't have seen it. The tiny gesture made her heart flip, and she looked down at her feet in embarrassment.

Chapter 15

Peter wasn't sure why he'd reacted so strongly to his brother's taunts. He usually enjoyed all his brothers' easy banter—especially when it wasn't aimed at him. He supposed it could be from a lack of sleep, but if he were being truthful, he would have to admit it was her. She'd affected him this way the other day too, but he'd hoped it was a fluke. Apparently not. Something about her sent his emotions into overdrive, and he had a strong feeling that she was more than she seemed.

He'd tossed and turned last night, trying to figure out why he'd been so rude around her, but all that had done was give him a headache and leave him tired and irritable. On top of that, he actually felt guilty, for no apparent reason. Argh, what a strange emotional state he was in. It baffled him. Even the Starling Trumpets weren't helping, and they usually did a wonderful job of soothing him.

Peter tried to ignore Jayne's presence, but it felt like the temperature of the room had changed where she stood, just off to his left, with her brother between them. The heat came at Peter like a furnace, but nobody else seemed to feel it. Peter focused on his brother and tried to sound indifferent, but he was failing if the looks Bryce and Damian were giving him were any indication.

Instead of staring at him as if he were mad, Jayne had giggled, which was annoying…and oddly endearing. He'd almost smiled, but then she'd looked down and the anger came back.

He let out a huff and turned to speak to her in what he hoped was a kinder tone than he'd used yesterday. "So, your brother said you have the next week free and that you're planning to get started on the translations."

Thankfully, it seemed he'd managed it, because she smiled shyly. "Yes, I hope that's okay with you. I'm really looking forward to getting the chance to help." She dropped her gaze again.

Her smile relaxed him again, and he sighed a little and smiled at her. "Okay. Let's go to the library then. I don't know if you need a reference point, but I'll show you where we started. Hopefully, that will give you an idea of the phonetics. They're a little different for us than the ones I've seen here so far." He started to turn away, but then Bryce spoke up loudly, clearly annoyed at not being properly introduced.

* * * * *

"Oi, stop hogging the attention, you fathead, and introduce me to this really pretty woman."

Again, Jayne thought of a petulant child, and she turned to him with a flash of temper. "My name is Jayne. No, I'm not deaf or here late for some scouting thing. I came to help Peter with some translations because I was invited to, and you're being very rude." She huffed then turned to see Peter bent over in silent laughter, tears streaming down his face, trying to breathe.

Her brother looked stunned but said nothing, his mouth hanging open and his hands frozen in mid-air as though holding onto something invisible.

Refugees

Bryce was shocked but recovered himself quickly and chuckled. "You've got spunk. I'm Bryce, one of Peter's older brothers." He stuck his hand out for her to shake. "It's nice to meet you. Sorry if I was being a bit of a jerk. Just teasing… You know how it is, right?" He shrugged and looked at her with a hopeful little smile.

She frowned at him, shook his hand, and turned without a backward glance, waiting expectantly for Peter to show her where the library was.

It took a minute for him to recover from his fit of laughter, and his eyes shone as he straightened up. "Right, let's get started, shall we? If you need a break at all, let me know. I often get side-tracked and forget to eat, so just speak up." He was still laughing, and he coughed and spluttered a little to clear his throat.

They chatted while walking away, leaving Bryce and Damian to stare after them. It wasn't as awkward as it could've been, which was a pleasant surprise. Today seemed to be full of surprises. Jayne absently wondered at her outburst but put it aside. She would look at that later, when she was alone and could analyse her moods privately. This was the first time she'd had a real outburst… Ever.

Chapter 16

Jayne and Peter went through the archway down a set of stone steps—there were clearly a few lower floors to this place, as the stairs descended several flights and had other hallways coming off them. Peter seemed to be in a better mood today, even though he kept rubbing his upper arm as though something was bothering him. She didn't say anything, just in case he got upset again. He seemed prone to mood swings, and she didn't want to jeopardise her chance to learn more about his culture. He seemed oddly quiet now that he was away from the others, and he kept glancing at her as though he wanted to speak.

"So, Bryce is your brother? He looks a lot like you and Jeff…" Was she being rude by asking?

He smiled a little. "Yes, Bryce is my eldest brother. I have twelve and I'm the youngest." He sighed a little, and her perfume engulfed him. It was a really delicate scent that reminded him of cinnamon with hints of vanilla and chocolate and biscuits. His tummy grumbled, and he smiled to himself with a little head shake.

"Are you hungry?" she asked in surprise.

"No, my stomach does that sometimes even if I'm not hungry," he said, but in truth his tummy never grumbled. It seemed to be a reaction to her. But he didn't want to say that.

She smiled at him. "So, you keep your library in the dungeon, huh? Should I be worried?"

Refugees

He chuckled. "No, I asked for a space that was quieter than the upper floors. It helps me think—and to be honest, I prefer the quiet. Upstairs gets real rowdy sometimes, especially if there's a feast or something. Everyone leaves me alone here." He shrugged and looked at her. "So, um, why is it that your hair and eyes are completely different?" He tried to sound only curious, but a hint of annoyance laced his words. He rubbed at his arm.

Luckily, she didn't seem offended. "Oh, didn't Dae tell you? I wear contact lenses and wigs so I can have a unique look every day if I want. This way I don't have to cut and dye my hair all the time, and my eyes can be whatever colour I want them to be. It's fun. Some people think I'm flat-out weird, but I don't really care much for their opinions."

"Hmm." He didn't want to be offensive, but he suspected he was one of those people. He really didn't understand why she wanted to look so different every single day. The people of Earth were so odd sometimes. Would there ever be a day when he wasn't surprised by them or learn new and strange facts about them? There were many positives, but some things seemed so…alien.

* * * *

They reached the bottom of the stairs and turned left again. The walls here were a simple cream colour and the few doors Jayne could see were all the same size and shape. After the third door they passed, Jayne let out another sigh. "This place is much bigger than I thought it would be. I mean, it looked big from the outside, but this is just incredible."

He made a sound that wasn't quite a snort and nodded. "Yeah, the building isn't actually this big. Even though our magix is limited, we can still do some stuff, so we enlarged the interior of the building to suit our needs. Did you notice that the doors upstairs are all different?"

She couldn't help gaping at him, but she managed to nod.

"Each door leads to a different environment. Not all of us stay here, but most do. The dragons have their own space so they don't have to be in human form too long. The Visper have a tranquil village surrounded by their native vegetation. The halls and meeting places are all neutral except for the one we were in earlier, and we use mass amounts of Starling Trumpets there for safety…"

When they reached the bottom of the stairs, Peter pushed open a set of heavy double doors and stood back to let her through. She only hesitated a moment and smiled a little when she passed him. Jayne stopped dead for the second time that day. The library was more like a cave—a very large, book-filled cave. Books were shelved in rows and along the walls. Over in a far corner, they were stacked like bricks in a tower. If she sat amongst them, she would be in a book fort.

* * * *

Peter watched her reaction with satisfaction. She really did love books, and it comforted him for some reason. How odd. He'd thought having her in his space would be uncomfortable, but she seemed to belong here. He sensed he'd made a friend, despite his mood swings.

* * * *

Jayne looked up at the gigantic man next to her. He was grinning with beautifully white, straight teeth, and she couldn't help but return it. It felt like they were scheming, like naughty children playing a joke on someone. This would be fun. Jayne

Refugees

loved translating, books, history, and mysteries, and Peter, it seemed, shared her feelings. After the other day, who would've thought they would have such a strong common interest?

Chapter 17

After showing Jayne around the library, Peter went to retrieve the samples so they could get started. He didn't know how helpful this would be, but he had to try everything. This so-called prophecy was the reason the Huntowra had started this war—yet Peter felt this was nothing more than an excuse. They wanted to kill everything, so eventually they would've started it anyway.

Thinking about what they'd done to start this, he wanted to rage and fight every last one of the Huntowra, yet he felt like he'd lost half of himself when he lost Lilah and then his sword Mirren only a few years afterwards. Talgra weapons contained the essence of magix from the greatest warriors and heroes, and without them, the Talgra lost motivation for fighting. The powerful weapons were drawn to their wielders and the connection grew as the weapon bonded to the wielder, becoming a sort of guide or mentor—sharing ancient traditions and information from their ancestors.

Making such a weapon required a special ritual and extensive amounts of power and preparation. It was the highest honour for the Talgra, and one of their greatest secrets—few outsiders knew of this, though the Aggaron and the Whistler were among those who did. Because of how few of these weapons existed, it was fairly uncommon to be gifted one. It happened in the ring—sometimes a weapon appeared along with the magix, meant for them. Technically nobody owned these weapons, but they stayed with their wielders for the

Refugees

entirety of their life, absorbing some of the wielder's magix and passing along the recent history to the next generations.

Peter's sword had come to him earlier, and though there was a lot of mystery and rumour around this, it had been generally accepted that this had happened because of Lilah. Peter sighed. Oddly, his heart didn't hurt, though it usually did when he thought about Lilah. This worried him some, but he pushed it away. He would figure it out another time.

He slowly made his way to and from various shelves, gathering books from the five different cultures as a starting point. When she had a grasp on each of these languages, he would show her what he was trying to decipher—which, as far as he could tell, was a weird cross between four, or maybe five, unique languages. He explained this to her as he laid the books on a heavy table.

* * * *

Jayne had to really work to concentrate on what Peter was telling her—that she would need to learn the basics of five distinct languages to be able to help decipher the texts—because he had such a soothing voice. It made her feel warm, safe, and completely at home. She pushed her thoughts aside and took the first book from Peter. The writings were like Egyptian hieroglyphs, and she could tell right away that this was a book of myths and legends.

They worked together for a few hours before Peter finally stretched and sighed. "I think I need to eat something. Are you hungry yet?"

"Yeah, actually, now that you mention it," she replied with a small yawn.

He smiled in answer and got up.

Jayne trailed him so she didn't get lost. It was a good thing she was feeling so well—all these stairs normally would've exhausted her. But, now that she thought about it…why was she feeling so well? She hadn't dwelled on her illness once today, yet it was normally all she could think about. She took a really deep breath in and exhaled slowly.

Peter eyed her curiously. "You okay?"

"Hmm? Oh yeah, I'm great, thanks. Just lost in thought." She gave a small, sheepish grin—she didn't want him to know about her mysterious illness. For now, at least.

* * * *

Peter frowned slightly but only gave her a tiny nod. It seemed there was something she wasn't saying, which frustrated him, but it wasn't his place to say anything. This thought made him suddenly sad—and then mad. Why the hell should he feel any of that, anyway?

When they finally reached the kitchen, Peter and Jayne set to making an enormous stack of sandwiches. Peter normally would've just magixed them, but Jayne had laughed at the suggestion and dared him to make them "the old-fashioned way". Not one to turn down a dare, and feeling oddly happy today, he set to work. Peter had to admit, it was much harder than he'd thought. He kept fumbling, unsure and not wanting to look foolish. In the end, he watched Jayne deftly chop up her salads and butter her bread. He copied her, pretending to know what he was doing.

* * * *

Jayne watched his clumsy efforts from the corner of her eye but decided not to say anything. He was trying and, from the look of it, learning. She felt a surge of pleasure that she'd

Refugees

taught him something, even if it was something as simple as making a sandwich. When they sat to eat, she swapped one of hers with his.

Chapter 18

She was quickly learning the basics of this language. It was a form of hieroglyphics, so similar it had to be related to the Egyptian system. But languages didn't spontaneously spring into existence—they began somewhere—and that they were so similar excited her. She could nearly use the same key to decipher the symbols, yet they were different enough to need further study. If she mistranslated even one tiny portion, the entire thing could have a completely different meaning. Which might be what had happened to Peter and all the others who'd tried to decipher the prophecy. If the way their magix taught them new languages relied on previous knowledge with the languages, perhaps it could make mistakes with a new language that had many similarities. Not that she was going to tell them that—she didn't think Peter would be too happy with her opinion on the matter.

She worked endlessly, getting lost in the familiar patterns of deciphering, and moving from one text to another so she was visualising each sample, processing it, and then allowing it to percolate while sampling another. Though he said nothing, Peter was watching her, seeming to be looking for a sign she was struggling. The thought gave her a sharp burst of uncharacteristic anger. The moment passed quickly, and Jayne forced herself to stop paying attention to the enormous man next to her.

She lost track of time then; the only sign that she'd been there any length of time was a tightness in her neck and

Refugees

shoulders. Jayne sat back and massaged her neck with her head tilted back and her eyes closed, enjoying the moment of rest. Peter suddenly appeared out of nowhere and set a cup of tea down next to her, along with a plate of biscuits.

She smiled at him a little ruefully. "Guess I got sidetracked. I didn't even notice you'd gone anywhere. Thanks for this."

He just studied her for a minute without saying anything. He took his time getting settled back in then looked at all the texts she'd been pouring over, clearly trying to see how she was doing.

Chapter 19

He frowned a little. "Do you really know how to translate?" he asked carefully. Surely she needed to focus on one text at a time. "I mean, you've been looking at these books randomly. There are four distinct languages here. They're not the same."

Surprisingly, she smiled at him. "I promise I know what I'm doing. This is a strange way to learn, but it works for me. I look at samples then while my brain processes them, I start on another one, and switch back and forth." Jayne sat quietly for a minute drinking the tea, while Peter thought over what she had said.

He had no idea how that could work; she was randomly picking up books and flipping through the pages, sometimes taking notes and other times looking at some of the books she'd brought with her. He'd watched her work for three hours before he went and got her some tea, and it had been strangely calming. He sighed to himself. Overall, she was a calm presence—there had been a moment of anger before, but she was undoubtedly just frustrated with the texts.

As she finished her tea, she took a deep breath and gave him an enormous grin that was undeniably smug. "Okay, so the first book I looked at is about the myths and legends of a race of people called Visper. They seem to be very shy but are amazing healers and farmers, from what I've been able to see so far. The myths are very gentle in that they don't have any war heroes or grand armies. Rather, they have these sort of spirit guides who help them harness their powers and learn their expert farming and building skills. Apparently, there was one guy named Herschel, who consulted the spirits and was told to build a village up in the trees because a great flood was coming. He was laughed at, but he went ahead and built enough dwellings up high for everyone in his village and stocked them with grains and seeds and food stuff. One night out of nowhere, a raging flood swept through and completely wiped out everything, but most of the villagers survived. So, thanks to Herschel, the whole village was saved. He became one of the greatest heroes of the Visper people." Jayne looked over at Peter and saw his shocked look, as though he couldn't believe what he was hearing. Clearly, he'd underestimated her ability. She felt smug as she began her explanation of the second book she'd looked at.

"The second one I've been working on is from a race of people called Aggaron. They're warriors and I get the feeling they idolise weapons. They ally with the strongest species they can find to trade with and stuff, except for a race called the Huntowra. According to the Aggaron, they're nothing more than locusts who need to be annihilated at all costs. They go on about them and how bad they are, how their greatest weapon is that they have wings. Anyway, this guide is kind of like an instruction manual on their weaponry and what it's used for. Proper war-like stuff, you know? This weapon kills that slug thing and so on…but you know what I don't get? I mean, they had all these weapons to fight these Huntowra, but nothing to stop them from being up in the air. I mean, that is their advantage, right? Couldn't they figure out a way to take away that advantage? So, like, here with our birds, if we don't want them to fly off, we clip one of their wings. Obviously, they can't clip their wings, but maybe there's another way." She shrugged.

"I just thought these super advanced, magical military dudes would've at least tried something…"

Chapter 20

Peter stared open-mouthed at Jayne. Take away their wings? Would that even be possible? Clearly, amazingly, she knew exactly what she was doing with the translations, but she'd also just offered up a novel idea to fight the Huntowra and seemingly had no idea how pivotal that could be in the coming war. Of course, she didn't *know* there was a war coming. All the cover stories were that their world had been damaged and needed extensive repairs, but they'd given no explanation as to what had caused the damage—most assumed it was weather.

"Hmm." He coughed slightly to get her attention. "I'm very impressed. You really know your way around languages. I'm sorry I questioned it before. And I'm also very impressed with your assessment of the Huntowra. So impressed, in fact, that I want to explain your idea to the council in the next meeting in two days."

"Okay." She looked at him with confusion. "Wait, why a council meeting? These texts are so old, I mean…they aren't still around, are they?" She nearly squeaked, her eyes bright with anxiety.

"Yes, sadly, they are. They've been at war with us for hundreds of years now. Mostly we get away with skirmishes and smaller battles, but occasionally they launch an all-out attack." He trailed off, letting the pain and frustration take him for a moment.

* * * *

His face was completely unguarded, transfigured with agony. This must be a horrific war, and he must've been affected by it personally. Only someone who'd suffered directly would react this way. Her heart broke a tiny bit for this gigantic man. She was surprised at how fiercely she wanted to hug him, to make everything right in his world. But that was nonsense. She could do neither, and it wasn't her place to, anyway. She had so many questions, but how could she ask them, given his obvious pain on the subject? She wanted to know all about this war. How had it begun? Why was it still going? Had there ever been any peace? Her questions must've been obvious on her face, because he answered them.

"There was never any peace once the war began. It was sad, really. The Huntowra, or who they were long before the war, were an incredible and kind race. Then over the course of about fifty years, a strange virus ravaged their world and it changed all the Huntowra who survived forever. Where once they were kind, they're now vicious. Their beautiful looks became deformed and demonic, and they only crave murder and war where once they ran from it and refused to fight. It's a sad, sad thing what happened to their species, but we can't allow them to continue as they are. Billions of beings are at risk, unfathomable numbers are dead. Entire planets have been annihilated by the Huntowra. The Aggaron were wiped out only twenty-five years ago in a full-scale attack." He was staring off into space and was barely audible as he continued, "They came one night while families were sleeping, went from house to house, and slaughtered every being in sight. Shortly after that, they attacked Meakra and Haven simultaneously. These two worlds were the next strongest, and staunch friends to the Aggaron and each other." His voice broke and he put up a hand to show he needed a minute before continuing, "They sent an elite assassin squad to Meakra and kidnapped their princess. We found out much later that they took her to a demon world called Qualterra and threw her to the immortal Shrogan. The demons ripped her apart, literally. She was only five years old." His voice broke again, and he got up and gathered the books together. Clearly, this hurt him greatly.

She needed to tread carefully, or he might refuse to answer any more questions. "Meakra, is that your world?" There was something about the name. It felt almost familiar, but she couldn't place why.

"No, I'm from Haven…but the princess was my best friend. It's hard to explain, but we were sort of, well, betrothed."

So this was the girl her brother had told her about. Of course he was crushed. Anyone would've been. She helped him put the books away without asking any more today. It was getting late anyway, and Dae would get worried if she stayed much longer.

Chapter 21

As Jayne and Peter slowly made their way back up the stairs to the primary meeting room, they spoke of more neutral things, like what would happen at the council meeting. He told her that it was likely the emperor of Meakra would want to meet her, and what the etiquette should be in that case: she shouldn't speak to him unless he spoke to her first, she wasn't to touch him, and it was rude to ask him any questions.

A sudden jolt of electricity ran through her, filling her with excitement but also nerves. She didn't want to offend anyone, but she honestly believed in treating all people as equals. Of course, she'd never met anyone royal before, and she supposed he deserved some respect for being the boss of an entire planet. That had to be a hard job. Had anyone ever spoken to the emperor the way they spoke to each other? It seemed almost sad if he hadn't experienced a normal conversation.

Peter chuckled then tried to cover it with a slight cough, causing Jayne to look at him in surprise. "He lived a very normal life with his wife and two children before becoming an emperor. He loves to invent things. That's actually what he wanted to do: invent new things to help his people and make life better for all." His expression was soft, and he looked down as he finished speaking, so he missed the look of shock on Jayne's face.

He'd answered her thoughts again. Her excitement left her at once, and she quietly asked, "Do all your people read minds?" She gave a tiny smile to show she was teasing him a

Refugees

little.

He looked shocked and frowned for a moment before responding. "No, it's actually very rare to be able to read another being's mind. I can't, though the princess could. You ask the strangest questions, you know. We were speaking of the emperor then suddenly you ask about telepathy. I'm intrigued by how your mind works." He looked a little wistful as he continued, "What's it like not being able to just magix anything? Life must be an adventure every day. We rely a little too much on our magix sometimes, I think." He shrugged and lapsed into silence.

"It isn't a glorious adventure for everyone. Very few actually get to do what they want because we have responsibilities and there are laws to follow. Wars break out over the stupidest stuff, and millions of people are starving and living on the streets, yet there's more than enough food and shelter for every human on the planet. We get greedy and become unkind to those less fortunate. We create new things to better everyone's lives then demand high prices for them, like, we have all these wonderful medicines and treatments to help save lives…but only if you have lots of money for it." She flushed pink. She was saying too much; this was too personal. Her own experiences with the medical system had made her passionate about the inequalities of the world. "Only some of us are lucky enough to live the life we want. For example, I can have my own bookstore and get to read and study and do all the things I love, but my friend Kayla is stuck doing part-time jobs when she can find them. She wanted to be a movie star, went to acting classes and everything, and she goes to every audition she can, but nobody will hire her."

* * * *

Peter had never considered that with all the bounties of this world there would also be darkness. Was this the price for such wonders? He had so much to learn about this world and couldn't use his magix to do so. He suddenly had an impression that he could spend entire lifetimes here and still never learn everything about Earth. The enormity and diversity of this world was staggering, even to him, and he'd seen so many worlds.

Some worlds were so small they could fit their entire population into one of the cities here on Earth, and others so large that the entirety of Earth's population wouldn't even fill one city, yet they all shared the same language and customs. If you spoke to one Visper then went to another village, they would speak the same language. Why was that? Even the few worlds with no magix were the same. Earth was completely unique for so many reasons. He loved mysteries, but sadly his curiosity about this world had to take a backseat to other, more pressing things.

Refugees

Chapter 22

Jayne looked up as they entered the meeting room. Her brother's voice was clear and excited, and he rarely sounded so happy. Taking on the role of breadwinner and caring for both Jayne and their mother had caused him to be much more serious than he should've been. It was lovely to hear his excitement, but what had caused it? He was sitting, surrounded by three men and three women.

She recognised Jeff and Bryant straight away. Another man was facing slightly away so she couldn't see his face properly, but he had to be another of Peter's brothers. A pretty woman with bronze hair in a tight braid had eyes that were the oddest combination of blue and grey, like liquid steel. She seemed bored, practically ready to get up and walk off. The next woman had tanned skin and straight hair that she wore in a simple ponytail at the nape of her neck. She was tall and willowy, accentuated by her tightly fitted jeans and top. A beautiful woman. The third woman was bubbly and energetic with light golden hair tumbling about her face and spilling down her back in loose curls. She wore a simple grey pencil dress and her skin was odd, almost shimmering—not pale but not tanned either. This was who Damian was talking to. They leaned toward each other as though nobody else existed in the world. Other conversations were happening around them, but they often had to be spoken to several times before they responded.

Damian looked up quickly then did a double take, and

nearly all the chatter stopped immediately.

"Sheesh, you don't have to get all quiet on my account," Jayne grumbled softly.

Dae laughed and his eyes sparkled. She couldn't help but be curious about it, though the woman with golden hair was clearly the reason.

The man who was turned slightly away continued to chat quietly with Jeff and the ponytailed woman. His deep voice was husky and sounded almost exactly like Peter's, except it was more...well, bouncy. This man was genuinely happy, whereas hurt laced Peter's words. Jayne marvelled at how easy it was to tell this, and she chuckled self-consciously. Apparently alerted by the sound, the man spun on the spot, his eyes locked straight onto hers, and Jayne's belly dropped through the floor.

She'd been prepared for the fact that Peter and his brothers looked so alike, but she'd had no idea that there were two Peters. After a moment, though, she could see the differences. His stance was more relaxed, for a start—except he held his arms crossed protectively across his chest, whereas Peter was always standing straight and tall, his arms swinging by his sides. His hair was the same length, but it fell down over his eyes a little, whereas Peter's hair was spiky and stood upwards. They both had spectacularly blue eyes, but Peter's were more intense and sometimes even chilling, while this other man had a sparkle to his.

Peter chuckled quietly next to her, and she let her gaze drift to him. He gave her a lopsided smile; obviously, this wasn't a new reaction to him. Jayne looked back to the other man, who gave her a rueful smile—which was also lopsided, but opposite to Peter's—and shrugged. He looked almost relaxed, but there was a sudden tightness in his jaw that told

Refugees

Jayne he wasn't quite as relaxed as he wanted everyone to think. After a moment, he blinked and shook his head a little, reached out his left hand slowly, and waited quietly for her to take it.

When she did, a zing of electricity shot up her arm, leaving goose bumps in its wake. He smiled again and nodded slightly, clearly assessing her.

"Hi, I'm Ethan."

The pretty girl with fitted jeans scoffed and pointedly looked away.

"I'm Jayne, Damian's sister. It's nice to meet you." She felt unaccountably shy talking to this man. Some of her confusion must've shown because Ethan examined her face then looked pointedly at the woman who was ignoring her.

"Jess, stop being childish, and introduce yourself." His voice was kind but there was a warning tone underneath it; he was angry and not bothering to hide it.

Jess took a deep breath and squared her shoulders, spun back to face them, and smiled—it was a very fake smile but at least she was trying. "Hi," she said in a high and false voice. "I'm Jess, and that's my cousin Emma." She pointed to the girl with steel eyes. "And that's my best friend Hannah." She poked her finger at the bubbly girl sitting with Damian.

Hannah cringed, Emma looked like she wanted to hit Jess, Damian seemed lost, but Ethan just rolled his eyes.

Jess didn't wait for Jayne to reply. She looked Ethan square in the face and snapped, "I'm going to get ready for Jye and the others' return. Angel will probably be exhausted, so if it's okay with you, I'll go now." She turned and stalked out of the room.

"Argh, she's such a bitch when there's competition around," Emma blurted. She grimaced and gave Jayne a tiny smile that was somehow a little aloof.

Not understanding anything that had happened here, Jayne simply smiled and pretended she hadn't noticed anything odd.

"She's upset because she has feelings for Ethan. Try not to take it personally. She's actually a really nice woman," Peter said reassuringly, again reading her thoughts. He'd tensed earlier, but he was back to himself now—as though something drastic had happened and now it was all better.

Again, Jayne simply nodded. There was nothing to say, really, and she hoped nobody expected her to find something.

Ethan gave his brother a strange and thoughtful look.

Peter shook his head slightly in response and looked at the stairway they'd just come from; clearly, he wanted to escape to his library again. She so got that. It had been a monumental day, she was exhausted, and she wanted to unwind with her beadwork in her big, comfy bed.

All the reading she'd done today had filled her head to the brim, and she couldn't figure out why some of the things didn't quite fit together properly. It was as though the languages that had been used were somehow jumbled up, and not just with the other languages. If that was the case, it was likely that the so-called prophecy had been completely misread or was even written in a code using multiple languages as a cipher. She wouldn't share these suspicions with Peter yet, in case he thought her a fool for it. Once she had proof, she would show him.

Dae gave her a look that clearly said he had noticed her

Refugees

confusion and would ask her about it later.

She gave him an affectionate nod.

Jayne was about to ask Damian if they should organise a barbecue, but she was distracted by the giant squared-off area. Transparent, glowing walls had appeared all around it, making a humming sound that reminded her of fluorescent lights. The circle in the middle also glowed a soft green, and the air felt charged with electricity. Jayne blinked to try to clear her head, but when she did, she felt sure that this wasn't the first time she'd seen this. One of her many weird dreams was so similar that adrenaline coursed through her.

She knew somehow what would happen next, and she couldn't look away, waiting for the arch to form and for someone to come through. It was like a tiny part of her brain had told her this was the way of it, and she accepted it without question. And sure enough, the arch began to form, the base widening out then reaching up gracefully, joining at the centre of the arch. A portal shimmered, rippled then solidified into something like a liquid doorway. Through the arch, people making their way to the doorway, and beyond them, there was a world of muddy red—so much red it looked like death.

A sudden chill went through her and she hissed softly under her breath, her mind screaming at her that this was a bad place. She took a few steps back until she bumped right into someone, her gaze still glued to the world beyond the doorway. The people walked through to the meeting room, but she watched the arch until it shrank away with the help of one of the men who'd come through. When it was completely gone, the walls fell and everyone started talking.

Jayne tried to concentrate on anything except her suddenly tumultuous emotions, looking at each person carefully and trying to focus on what they were saying. There were eight newcomers. One looked like another of Peter's relatives, even though his face and build were completely different to the ones she'd seen so far. He was pleasant to look at, about six-foot-tall and very proportionate, with grey eyes and pale skin that complemented his sandy brown hair. He smiled at Jeff and headed over toward the seat where everyone had been just a moment ago. The other four men weren't even remotely familiar. They were all tall and willowy with broad shoulders, inky hair, and eyes in varied shades of brown. They seemed completely at ease, as though nothing could ever faze or surprise them.

The three women were vastly different. One was a middle-aged woman with kind eyes slightly too big for her face and grey hair that escaped her bun. She smiled warmly at Jayne then stepped past her to hug Hannah. The next woman was also middle-aged, but she was exquisite with waist-length brown hair and a body almost as tiny as Jayne's. She had a surprisingly robust voice that carried clearly when she chided Ethan for not coming to get her the day before—but then she smiled ruefully, hugged the huge man, followed by all his brothers.

When she realised Jayne was practically standing on Peter's foot, she arched a delicate brow and pursed her lips. "Who's your lovely friend, Peter?"

"This is Jayne, Damian's little sister. She's here to help with the translations." He leaned around Jayne to hug the woman. "Jayne, this is my mother, Camilla. She loves singing more than reading, which I'm sure you'll hear all about soon enough."

"Hello," was all she could say.

Camilla stared at her for another moment then clapped

Refugees

her hands. "I'm going to get some food. It's been a long and hot trip, so which of my handsome sons will walk with me?"

From behind her, the other woman spoke in a voice like an angel's. "Oh, that sounds rather lovely, Milly. I think I'll join you. These treks really take it out of me." She smiled softly but fidgeted with her hands, looking curiously at Jayne.

Jayne must've been more exhausted than she'd realised because, for some reason, she got a very cold feeling when this woman looked at her. She was beautiful, with long, wavy, sand-coloured hair, ice-blue eyes that sparkled, and a full mouth tinted a pale rose. She wasn't carrying any of the numerous bags, so it seemed she was an important person.

"Hi," she said to the woman quietly. Everything about her made Jayne feel defensive.

"Yes," was all she answered, a clear dismissal. Her eyes were suddenly very cold and narrowed in anger, her mouth flattened into a grimace. After a moment, the woman walked right past Jayne, seeming almost to float.

Peter called out to her, "Angel, is everything okay? It's not like you to be so quiet." His voice held genuine concern, and Angel paused.

After a taking a deep breath, she answered softly, "I think I'm just tired. Sorry if I seemed rude to your friend, Peter." She reached out behind her, though she didn't turn or look at any of them, and Peter took her hand and held it for a moment.

When he let it drop, she simply walked away.

It stayed with Jayne, the way Angel had pushed her hand back while looking in the opposite direction. There was something chilling about it, or perhaps it was because her hands looked like slimy spiders, much too long to be considered normal. Another shiver skittered down Jayne's spine.

Refugees

Chapter 23

Five Huntowra, known as the Elite Five, were feared above all others. The assassin squad held the highest ranking of all Huntowra—apart from the queens, of course—and could work solo or as a team. They were different to other Huntowra—most needed to follow, but the Five led. Their names were reverently whispered, they were so feared.

There were days of recognition for the Five, as there were for the queens. In lesser species, these days were marked with feasts and celebrations, but the Huntowra marked theirs with battles. The queens were brutal and they each ruled over their territory with a mighty hand. Aside from not dishonouring your clan by dying, there were no other rules and you were free to challenge whoever you wished. Young Huntowra often spoke of challenging a queen. Those who were foolish enough to do so rarely lived, and it wasn't in the queens' natures to show mercy, but mostly it was just bluster and bragging.

Only one queen was never present, and no Huntowra dared speak her name. She was so feared even the other queens trembled at her mention. The oldest and strongest of the Five was the only one to ever speak of her with reverence instead of fear. He alone answered directly to her, the queen other queens feared, and she trusted him with the most vital of information. He'd been trained by her hand, and the queens were in agreement that she was the most brutal and bloodthirsty creature of all. He was a twin, almost completely unheard of for Huntowra, but the twin wasn't trained or favoured the way he'd been. Nosk had sparked legends with his brutal history, and the other Five all looked to him as their leader.

He didn't like sitting still. Inaction made him want to murder and set his companions in competition with each other. Nosk wanted to be out there doing his bit for his species, cleansing the path for all Huntowra to live free with no real threats or lack of worlds to seed. Only he and his mistress knew the truth: they needed to win this war and time was running out to do so. In another century, the Huntowra would face extinction. Unless they could safely seed the life-giving vines that birthed all Huntowra, the plant would die and no more could be born of it. If the others discovered this, there would be riots and clan wars, they needed to focus on fighting their enemies in order to succeed, not fight with each other.

The queens weren't just brutal, they were ignorant beings who wanted only bloodshed, yet his mistress wanted more: to thrive, to have larger worlds safe for spawning. That was the challenge—the climate and ground had to be exactly right, and they needed to be able to absorb magix, of course. There were a few perfect worlds. There was an unnamed but vast and vibrant world, however it was heavily populated by behemoths—large worm-like creatures with no eyes that used their magix to detect the presence of others. They didn't seem to have any weakness either. They were a parasitic, unintelligent species, laying eggs inside each other that ate their way out when it was time for birth. They destroyed each other as much as other species, burrowing and attacking whenever they felt the desire to do so, causing enormous cracks in the ground as they went. The entire surface of the planet would shake, and liquid fire spewed from mountains whenever one burrowed too far down.

Refugees

It had been on this world that the first of the Huntowra had spawned, but they'd moved once they became sentient enough to want to live. The behemoths spewed out magix-infused goo that sucked a being dry of magix then they ate it. The being was crushed in the process—accidental and unavoidable. The goo left magix deposits on the plant life, infusing the vines with magix. Over time, the plants seeded, and this was how the first of the Huntowra had emerged, born fully grown.

There were still seeds from the origin world. They were rare and hidden from even the other queens, who'd wiped out as many of the seeds as they could in an attempt to be titled the strongest queen. As the queens' strength grew so did their clans, and their control over the minds of their clans, but they were power hungry and always wanted more. The idea that they would have to share with yet more potential queens infuriated them.

Nosk and his mistress hoped to seed them on alternative worlds, keeping them hidden until they were mature enough to handle being attacked by other beings, or queens. They hoped the vines would take, and quietly absorb the magix around them, allowing new Huntowra to spawn.

The virus that had made the Huntowra as they were today was also slowly killing the vines. The only thing he didn't understand was how nobody else could see this plain truth. His mistress had laughed when he queried it, and said it was because they two of them had been born during the first infection. Though they had the brutality of their kind, they could also reason and predict, and still felt positive emotions. That clashed with their brutal new natures and caused them physical pain but added to their overall strength.

Nosk's twin wasn't the same though. Leinad was more brutal than other Huntowra, but his brain was only wired to kill. Despite this, Mistress had instructed Nosk to train him anyway. It wasn't the specialised and intensive training he'd received, but his mistress had watched from the shadows and instructed him in the ways she wanted Leinad trained.

He was her recon soldier, her spy, stealthy and strong, and unique in that the other queens couldn't read his thoughts. It had made it hard for Leinad to gain the trust of a queen, but he had, and he'd been reporting back ever since. His queen, Etta, wasn't as suspicious as the others and curious about his mind, which made her the perfect target to monitor the others and feed them information and falsehoods to prevent all-out war. Leinad knew his job was vital but not why, and Mistress was pleased he was so accommodating with so little fuss.

She'd worked tirelessly to set up this war, doing everything from planting spies, killing off dead ends, finding targets that were key to giving the Huntowra every advantage, and even implanting herself in the midst of their enemies. She'd glamoured herself to look the opposite of her true self, which also made her magix feel different. He shuddered with revulsion as he drank his ale while watching his brother and other companions.

Leinad wrestled with Kyden, the newest of the Five. He was easily the next strongest Huntowra, but Leinad was quicker and could spot openings in a fraction of a second, allowing him to sneak in extra jabs. It seemed that Bane was also interested in playing. He slowly worked his way to where Leinad now had Kyden by the throat and was trying to choke him, while Kyden flipped over and over, weakening the hold on his neck. Both were snarling and yelling at each other, unintelligible words

Refugees

designed to infuriate and enflame their brutal natures.

Kyden was arrogant and cocky, always bragging about his position and ability. But if it hadn't been for his clan's queen Odessa killing off the other strong Huntowra of her clan in a fit of temper, Kyden wouldn't have been selected as a member of the Five. The other members of squad never let Kyden forget it either. He was a perfect target for their tormenting, and he often found himself in trouble. His inability to remain focused was one of his biggest weaknesses, as was his quick temper. So whenever they ganged up on him, he would want to fight, prove he was the best and strongest. Today, Bane was the one who set things in motion. After watching Kyden and Leinad, he shoved Kyden roughly in the back, snickering at him.

Nosk watched them apathetically. He had much more important matters on his mind right now. His mistress hadn't contacted him recently, even though she was on a world where she could do so. What if their enemies were realising she was among them, sabotaging their war efforts, warning the Huntowra of known attacks whenever she could without giving herself away?

His mistress would leave a message in plain sight, and he or his brother would pass them along as needed. Sometimes it was a simple symbol etched into a wall or tree, and other times it was a subtle hint of magix infused into some ordinary object that would be easily overlooked. The messages had no words, but he understood the code. An etching on a log meant something different to an etching on a footpath or wall, and infused objects meant something different as well, depending on whether they were natural or crafted. Sometimes he would pick up an object, and a flash of memory would blind him, letting him know that a very serious threat was near while still protecting their secrets. If another were to pick up the object, they would only get a blinding headache and become confused.

But he'd received no messages on his last scouting trip. He sighed and switched his attention back to the fight. At least it was something to do until he got his next task.

* * * *

Bane swung hard at Kyden and knew straightaway that the blow would connect. He was faster and knew Kyden's moves and ploys better than anyone. He aimed slightly lower and to the left because Kyden favoured this avoidance manoeuvre as a result of a beating he'd received as a young Huntowra. He'd nearly died when his queen heard him brag about his abilities. Admittedly, he was the only one to ever survive that particular queen's rage, but it left him with deep scars on his back, arm, and leg. Even his left wing was scarred and permanently bent.

Odessa had crushed his whole left side, and then, thinking he'd died, had ordered the others to place him under an enormous boulder and encouraged others to visit his rotting carcass—a sign of shame and dishonour. Strong Huntowra who died with honour were buried fully. He'd torn his scalp away at the back and down his left shoulder almost to his waist, and his left side was weaker than the right as a result of him ripping his way out from under the boulder that was supposed to be his shameful tomb.

Kyden had stormed right back into Odessa's domain and boldly asked to be pardoned. It had sent shockwaves throughout the Huntowra, and news of his actions spread to the other queens. Eulalia and Cordelia had stepped in and demanded that she do so, for he'd returned and showed her loyalty and respect, even after he'd been shunned and shamed

Refugees

for no real reason other than that she'd felt like it. They'd reminded her that he'd in fact survived the attack, a feat none other could claim, and so he became the first Huntowra welcomed home by his queen, and also the first to be under the protection of two other queens from his own queen's wrath. They were each attempting to win him over to their clans, but he was stubborn and refused to betray Odessa.

If Bane ever hoped to win Nosk's respect, he had to be better than everyone else. Nosk had saved him, had shown him the genuine power of the Huntowra and what they were capable of. He wanted to be just like Nosk: fierce, with a strong mind. Bane had killed more than the others, except for Nosk, of course. It was a fun sport, hunting weaker and lesser beings down, torturing them, only killing them when they begged to die—very slowly and with no remorse.

Bane wanted nothing more than to skin Kyden alive, to hear him scream in agony and see him bleed. Nosk had refused to allow this, of course, so he picked fights with Kyden instead. When this war began in earnest, though, he would kill Kyden and no Huntowra would ever find his rotting carcass. He would simply be gone. After a time, nobody would even remember him or his story, pathetic cur. He had no right to be a Five. His only strength was that he'd lived, yet that wasn't heroic—he'd simply failed to die when sentenced to do so.

His own past had been far worse, and yet he'd earned his position here with his skill. Nosk had found him surrounded by hundreds of Aggaron scum and saved him. He'd plotted to kill a handful of them, but it had gone horribly wrong, as things sometimes do. He'd been prepared to die that day, yet it seemed like the universe wanted him alive. Nosk showed no fear when facing them, slaughtering all but one small boy to spread the legend. Nosk's might and courage had served as a glorious awakening, showing Bane that he was truly the most powerful Huntowra. He'd vowed then to always stand next to his hero, to learn from him and one day, maybe, be praised by him.

Bane watched smugly as Kyden ducked to the left at the last second and his punch connected. Kyden stepped back, holding his jaw as his expression turned murderous. Bane's wings flexed in anticipation, giving a small shudder of delight. Kyden didn't disappoint; he started swinging his fists furiously and bellowing like a wounded Shrogan. This battle wouldn't last, though. In a few moments, Kyden would recover himself and storm off to get into mischief elsewhere and, hopefully, stay out of Bane's way for a few weeks. It was so predictable that even a hatchling could've seen it, yet it was still amusing.

The Huntowra were best suited to long-range, aerial combat, where they had the advantage and could feel when magix was shifting in a new direction. Hand-to-hand was reserved only for days of remembrance and gatherings, but it was worth the pain in his right arm to have hit Kyden. Bane's split-second preoccupation gave Kyden an accidental opening, and he drove his right arm into Bane's chest, knocking him into a bunch of strangers behind him. Kyden boomed out a laugh, a performance meant to draw everyone's attention, and Bane looked instinctively towards Nosk, but he was nowhere to be found.

A moment of panic rose within him. Bane had thought from watching earlier that Nosk was interested in the quarrel. He'd believed Nosk had been amused and had wanted to be the one to entertain him. Now, though, he wondered if that were the case. Perhaps Nosk had simply grown weary and left for the time being, or perhaps his queen, the monster no Huntowra

Refugees

dared speak of openly, had called him to her. It saddened and angered him, so he decided to leave the gathering place and find something to hunt.

He exchanged taunts and glares with Kyden, who'd sulked like an infant, then left, feeling savage pleasure at Kyden's discomfort.

* * * *

Kyden hated that Bane had riled him so easily. His temper had always been his biggest weakness. He'd actually expected Bane's attack to his left side and allowed it, because he needed to remain the bumbling fool they thought him. Soon enough, though, he would show them all.

When Odessa nearly killed him, placing his body in a pose of shame, he'd felt rage like he'd never known—but what had happened after…well, that was what made him special. He was linked with three queens now. Though only Cordelia was aware of it, he was a spy for her, passing on intel from Odessa and Eulalia. He wanted Odessa dead. She was known for her temper tantrums, and Eulalia protected and defended her repeatedly. Cordelia would slaughter them both, take their territories, and be the most powerful queen—apart from the one Nosk answered to, of course. He would be indispensable, Cordelia's trusted assassin. Essentially, he would be the new Nosk.

These thoughts calmed his mind, and he sulked off to the booth farthest back from the door, where he sat with six others. This was his true purpose here. He'd known the others would provoke him then leave, giving him peace to meet his new team. For three years, after every attack, he'd sulk around and whisper with small groups. The rest of the Five used to watch closely, but now it meant nothing to them, which was exactly how he wanted it.

Refugees

Chapter 24

Feeling content, Kyden settled in to talk with the others. They had plans to lay, and he didn't want to dawdle now. They'd been watching the Talgra teams in the Qualterra and noticed patterns to their tracks. They could now confidently predict where and roughly when they would be in the valley of caves, it was a challenging area to set up a trap but not impossible. It also provided shelter if a storm brewed—essential since storms disadvantaged the Huntowra. The rain on Qualterra was like acid and lightning strikes were frequent.

The next team's trip wasn't ideal because it was still in storm season, but the one after that would be perfect. Which meant they had five weeks to set up, practice manoeuvres, and make any adjustments needed to give them every possible advantage. They would head into the valley two days before the group was due then set up the traps and place food caches in several safe areas, spanning a fifty kilometre range. This gave the prey lots of running room, but Kyden didn't mind; he enjoyed an excellent hunt.

What did worry him was that this plan meant he would be land-based. He was better in the air, especially now that he had scarring and weakness in his left side. Though he was sure the Talgra didn't know, they weren't the only ones he had to worry about. For the last few months, he'd noticed his colleagues watching his interactions with the other Five members closely, and he was thankful he'd played up his limitations. They thought him the bumbling and trusting fool, and that would be their failing in the end.

In truth, he needed numbers, these Huntowra were expendable, and he felt no remorse that some of them would die soon. This ambush would prove that he could take on missions without his assassin brethren behind him. As a lesser of the Five, he wasn't trusted to set up and execute a plan of this magnitude without the others, so this would show them all. Plus, he would gain more of Odessa's trust—an added bonus because the closer he got the easier it would be to discover her weaknesses for Cordelia.

When he was finished here, he would go and sulk on his own as he'd been doing for the last few years, and when he was sure there were no other beings around, he would get a message to his true queen then check the valley for potential problem areas with his own eyes. He didn't want to chance these upstarts taking him by surprise. He was hoping for the opposite: that he would have a few traps set for them so when the time came he could be rid of them *and* his targets.

Chapter 25

Bane took his rage to the nearest inhabited world and searched for a new target. The hunt would make him feel better. He watched with sharp eyes, looking for the one that stood out. These beings weren't his favourite species to hunt—they died too quickly and the rush wasn't as good as with the more aggressive beings—but they would do for now. He looked out into the sea of nervous, blue-tinged faces with overlarge, glowing eyes. Cowards. They were always hiding from other species instead of fighting to save their own kind, and it made him want to vomit.

He'd encountered the natural predators of this world on his first visit here. It had almost cost him his leg, but he'd escaped the creature and had no interest in hunting its kind either. They were just mindless beasts happy to go about their own business, leaving him free to do as he pleased, provided he stayed out of chewing range. He'd set up his hide in the tall trees of their territory, which the cowardly beings stayed well clear of. He was full from feasting earlier and comfortable enough to sit and wait patiently. This was not the best part for Bane, but it was just as important to select the right target.

He watched as a mother played on the grass with her younglings surrounded by dozens of other families all doing different activities in the cool evening air. The suns had set, but the luminous glow of several lanterns lit up the parkland and surrounding huts. Cobbled roads wove paths amongst them like a giant web and tiny pops of light told him more lanterns had been lit along the paths, no doubt to ensure the safety of the world's native people. Maybe he should just go pick a fight with a Shrogan. At least then he'd have to work up a sweat. Bane watched for days, but in the end none of these beings interested him enough to hunt, so he quietly left in search of another target.

He went first to a woodland world that used to be home to a small dragon population, but there was no worthy prey so he moved onto the next—the world where he'd first met Nosk, Helios. It was where the Aggaron had been slaughtered. A tiny shiver ran through him. He enjoyed those memories and relived them while wandering aimlessly. Occasionally, other warriors came here, perhaps looking to find weapons or see if any Aggaron had survived. He couldn't blame them, really, for hoping—the Aggaron had been an excellent race of warriors, after all—but after the battalions of Huntowra had come through, the Five had tracked all remnants of the race and slaughtered them. There were no survivors.

In front of him and slightly to the right, a shadow danced across the ruins of a wall. Someone was here. Instantly on alert, he looked for a vantage point. He found a crumbling tower that had a three-hundred-and-sixty-degree view and silently made his way up to look for the source of the shadow. After a quick search, he found movement that soon proved to be a warrior dressed in unfamiliar clothing. He didn't recognise the species, but the man wore weapons similar to ones used by the Aggaron, yet he was sure this wasn't an Aggaron. A frown furrowed his brow. The man acted as though he'd never come across a Huntowra before, walking around with no fear whatsoever. How was this possible? He'd heard that the Talgra and Whistler were attempting to recruit new warriors, but he never thought they would find ones from somewhere unknown.

Refugees

His wings fluttered and tapped what was left of the archway, knocking a stone loose. The noise when the stone hit the ground echoed in the otherwise silent world, and the strange man spun quickly, raising his weapon and scanning the ground with a beam of light coming from one of his hands. His whole being had changed; he was no longer casually wandering but was as alert and sharp as Bane. This was his prey. This strange being had sharp instincts and a killer look about him. He would make a fine kill.

Bane continued to watch as the man checked in and around corners. He had something on his eyes and was murmuring to himself. What a strange creature. The man continued to murmur as he walked around several old buildings then at last he seemed reassured and went back to his original spot, leaning against the old wall section and muttering to himself before lapsing into silence. Bane didn't understand the language at all, which should've been impossible. All beings relied on magix to help bridge the barrier between languages, and the only species they couldn't communicate with were the Shrogan—who'd never spoken, seeming to prefer to communicate with gestures—and the Huntrah, who'd gone extinct centuries ago, taking all knowledge of their language with them.

Cautious, curious, Bane settled down to watch.

Chapter 26

Seth felt like his heart had jumped into his eye sockets. Something had moved, he was sure of it. He'd swept the area but found nothing, so he went back to his post and checked in with Travis, his team leader. In all the time they'd been coming here, they'd never encountered any animals—not even a rat, or whatever passed for a rat here—so he knew he was being watched. Travis had told him to play it up. The only ones who came here apart from the scouts were the Huntowra. If they got lucky, they could catch one.

They'd faced them enough to know the personality type—the smash-and-grab, brute-strength-of-a-bear kind. There weren't any real thinkers among the Huntowra, except for the elite Five, who were supposedly the worst and strongest of them all, apart from the queens, and he very much doubted they would hang around this place. Huntowra were predators by nature and preferred hunting grounds rich with prey, so coming here was always left to the weak and unimportant—according to everything they'd learned anyway.

No one on Earth could understand the Huntowra language. It was very strange, and for some reason, they didn't use the translation trick the other species did. Jye, his Talgra friend, had explained that they could only translate if they had a reference point to start with, and the Huntowra had encountered no species with enough similarities to make the connection yet. Soon enough, they would, though, and then they would automatically slip into using Earth's languages without

Refugees

realising it.

The scouts kept getting sent here to check if there were any survivors, and they'd had a few close encounters with the Huntowra, so the A.S.U figured after a while that this would make a great place to catch some of them and see what their plans were, study their weaknesses. They used the Talgra and Whistler to translate when interrogating a Huntowra, but they'd gotten little from them yet. They had strength but didn't know how to use it effectively in a fight. Instead, they relied on their instinct to go high, and Seth was having a hard time not looking up. He'd been trained well, but his acting skills were crap and he worried he would somehow give himself away. It seemed his lame attempt had worked, though; there was no reaction from his stalker.

He knew the drill: act nonchalant then carefully lead his target towards the old city centre, a maze of buildings and skyscrapers with stained glass windows telling stories of the planet's history. It was a brilliant place to ambush an enemy, especially since it took away the advantage of flight. There just wasn't enough wing space for an air attack, so they would have to land, which was a weakness for them.

When they'd destroyed this world, it had been a combination of using overwhelming numbers, sneaking around when everyone was sleeping, and lots of planning. It had likely taken them several years to plan and coordinate so that every last one of the Aggaron was slaughtered at the same time. The queens knew their stuff, and the hives followed directions with no questions or thoughts of disobeying. It made them a dangerous foe, but they never knew how to react in an emergency situation. They couldn't think 'on the fly' and didn't deviate from their limited tactics for any reason, even if it meant death.

After a few more minutes, Seth swept his area again, humming a tune under his breath so it appeared he was still talking to himself. He walked around the entire block then headed up to the city centre, where his team was getting into position to catch this big, ugly bird. Up ahead, there were some trees with sweet-smelling flowers that reminded Seth of marshmallows roasting. He didn't know their name but wished he could take some home with him. It wasn't allowed, of course, with the strict quarantine laws, but he still wished anyway. The trees formed a sort of border for the city, separating the buildings from the suburbs and farms tightly packed like neat little bricks of land.

Seth was looking at his feet, deliberately walking slowly. He got the signal via his earpiece that the trap was ready and coughed to let his team know he'd heard it. As he made his way into the tree line, Seth felt something odd, a breeze in the windless night. He was about to radio Travis when there was a sharp blow to his skull then nothing.

In his semi-conscious state, he knew he was being moved, and there was an odd sound, like a rhythmic beat that seemed to intensify then die out before coming back again. For a moment, light bled through his closed eyes, but then he passed out.

When he next came around, his body dropped and pain erupted. His head throbbed and stung. His arms felt heavy and cold at the wrists. His legs were fine, though, and his mind was clearing. He obviously wasn't on the same planet anymore, otherwise he would still hear Travis or the others through his earpiece. That was bad, but he needed to focus. He opened his eyes a sliver to see if there was any way to escape, or if there

Refugees

was some kind of object he could use as a weapon.

He was in a shabby stone room. The walls were half his height, chipped and covered in vines, and the ceiling was arched like a gothic cathedral. The floor was stone as well, with columns all around. He couldn't see beyond the walls, it was too dark, but the air here was still and eerily quiet. He looked down at his hands. A thin chain was wrapped around his wrists, rusted and fragile-looking. His captor was either very sure he wouldn't escape or that he could prevent Seth from getting too far. Probably the latter. So how would he escape?

He had nowhere to go, but if he hid and waited, he might get rescued. The others would get backup, and the Talgra and Whistler would be able to track the magix. All he had to do was not die. Plus try to find out why he'd been taken, since the Huntowra never took a hostage without a reason. If only he could've understood the language; at least then he might've gotten some useful information while he waited for rescue.

An almost inaudible shuffle behind him alerted Seth that he wasn't alone. He turned slightly and saw the outline of his captor. He was shorter than Seth, maybe five and a half feet tall with a medium build, almost stocky but not quite. The darkness completely obscured his hair and eyes, but they were clearly dark-coloured as well. The Huntowra appraised him for a moment then a low, menacing growl escaped its mouth. The sound snapped Seth out of his thoughts and he instantly stood straight up, refusing to back down because he was chained like a dog.

"You stupid bastard, I'll never tell you anything so get on with it already," he spat.

The Huntowra just stood there, clearly not understanding, though it must've been obvious from his expression and tone that Seth wasn't scared. After a moment of thought, the Huntowra seemed to understand that Seth wouldn't cower or plead, and he lashed out with his right fist, smashing it into Seth's ribcage. A loud crack echoed in the silence, and Seth bit his lip hard to keep from crying out. He wouldn't show how much he hurt; it was part of his training, no matter what, he would stay as quiet as possible for as long as possible. Breathing raggedly, he straightened and glared at his captor again.

* * * *

Bane smiled. This whelp would be a wonderful trophy. Perhaps he would toy with him a while longer than usual—this one wouldn't give in easily, and that excited Bane. It had been almost a year since he'd found prey this stubborn. That one had lasted nearly two weeks. Bane couldn't understand this creature's words, but he would know when it had reached its limits and then he would kill it, slowly. He would start with beatings then move on to electrocution. Burning. Cutting. If he made it past these, if he refused to beg for death, he would skin the creature alive, slowly. He would use the ashan root to keep the creature alive when the last strip of flesh was peeled away from his body. He sometimes left his prey right there, skinless so it would die shamefully and alone, but perhaps with this one, he would deliver him back to his people—then he could watch their agony and grief as well.

Bane lashed out at the man again, connecting just under the shoulder, and this time the arm bone snapped under his fist. His own hand hurt from the force behind the punch, but it didn't bother him; he was used to pain. He continued his attack, calculating the best places to hit, but the man didn't scream. He whimpered a few times and his lip was bleeding from biting it.

Refugees

It was impressive. He hadn't thought the creature would be this strong.

Chapter 27

Seth was beyond wanting to cry out now. He'd been beaten so badly, and yet his captor hadn't tried to communicate with him, which meant he wasn't looking for information. But what did he want then? What was with the calculated beating? It didn't really make much sense right now, but he was still alive and that was a start. His hope of being rescued sustained him when the panic and pain threatened to overtake him—though if he would still feel this way in another day or so was debatable, assuming he even survived that long. For now, he'd been left alone and that gave him time to think. He tried to stay focused but the longer he was alone, the more panic set in.

The Huntowra came back after what seemed like a few hours, and he had some plants, bowls, and water with him. Uh oh. Not good. If he was bringing stuff to sustain life, he clearly wasn't finished with whatever it was he was doing, Seth cringed and then winced in pain at the thought. The Huntowra eyed him carefully for a moment then set about mixing some water and plants together into what looked like terrible porridge; it was gluggy, a muddy color, and smelled sort of like liquorice.

After mixing and grinding the stuff, he forcefully grabbed Seth's head, tipped it back, and slowly poured the liquid into his mouth. Seth spat it out, and the Huntowra squeezed his jaw tighter and snarled viciously in his face, and Seth didn't need to understand his language to hear the threat. He either ingested the stuff or got another round of beatings.

Refugees

Seth debated for a fraction of a moment if he should just let the thing beat him again, but then he remembered his team and his friends. If he didn't make it out alive, at least they would know he tried to survive for as long as possible.

He opened his mouth and let the gluey mixture be poured in. It wasn't the worst thing he'd eaten; it was a little like the cold, gritty porridge Nana used to shove down his throat, but it left him with a stinging burn that reminded him of the dentist. The flavour was a weird cross between aniseed, dirt, and flour. He gagged it all down then waited for whatever was coming next…but the Huntowra just left. Why was he doing this?

* * * *

Bane needed to let the man rest for a day or so, so he went to a nearby river and washed up, taking his time cleaning the blood and dirt off. The man's internal injuries weren't life-threatening, but it was better to be safe. If he died now, it wouldn't be as fun, and he'd need to find new prey sooner. Though he was looking forward to watching his people's pain when he dumped the creature's body.

He'd gotten the idea when Nosk rescued him, leaving one alive to spread the word of his deeds. Bane wanted to be as feared and respected as his hero, so he'd decided he would take mementoes from each victim then dump them back where he'd captured them—in this way signing his work so the lower beings knew it was him. His brethren were already telling stories of a rogue Huntowra so powerful he couldn't be caught, even questioning if he would be stronger than Nosk—an honour that made him eager to continue his work.

And it was important work. He needed to cleanse the worlds of the filth that plagued them so his brethren could spread out. More territory for each of the queens meant more Huntowra and stronger hives. Whoever had the strongest hive was revered as godly—something the queens all wanted more than the eradication of life. The only exception to this was Nosk's queen...Legna. He shuddered at the thought of her name then went to find something to kill for his evening meal.

* * * *

Seth was dizzy and numb, his limbs filled with lead, undoubtedly a side effect of the plant gunk he'd been fed. He had a high tolerance for anaesthetics—where they quickly knocked out other people, they only sedated him for a short time—and this sedative seemed to work about as well as a local anaesthetic. He could use this to his advantage. The Huntowra clearly thought he couldn't move, since he'd left him here. This was the moment. Thanks to this plant in his system, he felt minimal pain.

He would break the rusted chain, find some shelter somewhere, and hope for a rescue. He rolled to his belly and slowly got to his feet then turned in a circle, each turn tightening the chain a little more until it got so tight he could no longer stand properly. Seth tugged upwards, the chain started to let go then, with a tiny *pop,* he was free. His hands were still shackled together, but the chain holding him to the floor was broken.

He looked around. The setting sun was almost gone, so he had to hurry now. There was a forest on one side of the stone room, and the Huntowra had walked off in the other direction earlier. Not liking either option very much, he desperately looked behind him then started running as fast as he could toward a high cliff face, with enough tree cover that he would be hard to spot from above. Seth didn't look back even as he slowed to a fast hobble. He'd trained in harsh conditions and

Refugees

loved bush walking, but in this terrain, it was more like mountain climbing.

He made it to the tree line and started looking for shelter. He didn't think the Huntowra would come looking on foot but didn't want to make it too easy for him if he did. Seth kept moving. He didn't know how long the gunk would keep his pain levels down. He wound his way through the trees slower than before. There were loose rocks scattered all round, and he had to concentrate on where he stepped. With his hands shackled, if he fell over, he wouldn't be able to catch himself, so he needed to be even more careful than usual. Eventually, he stopped altogether.

He'd been walking for about an hour and scanned the cliff face again. It was almost dark. From this close, he could see pockets near the base of the cliffs, almost like shallow caves. There were dense bushes covering parts of the cliff so if needed, he could probably hide in them. He headed to a larger-looking nook as the darkness set in. The temperature was mild so he doubted he would die from exposure, but there didn't seem to be any water around, which would be a problem if he was here for longer than a day or two. There were some berries on the surrounding bushes though.

They looked okay to eat, so he grabbed a handful then stopped and squinted at the cliff face. The angry shadow had an even darker shadow. He crouched down for a better look. Behind the bushes there was a small hole, almost at ground level and big enough for maybe two people to crawl into. He shone his torch in. It was like a tube, going in about six feet then opening further back.

He pocketed the berries he'd picked and crawled in using his forearms. The pain was still bearable, so he let himself relax a little. The Huntowra wouldn't be able to follow him in; his wings were too big to fit through the entrance. Seth silently thanked his lucky stars and slowly made his way in further. There was no sound in here. He listened and got himself as ready as he could to backtrack if there was a critter hanging around, but he didn't see anything in the torchlight.

The tube opened into a cavern big enough for twenty people, with veins running off in different directions. None of the other tubes looked any bigger than the one he'd come in through. After relieving himself, he gathered some leaf litter as a makeshift, and mostly useless, bed and settled himself as best he could.

He got the berries out of his pocket and gingerly ate one. It was tart as a lemon but full of juice and better than nothing at all, so he quickly chomped down the rest. He might get sick from them, but at least he wasn't still chained up and being beaten. He switched off his torch, not wanting to waste the batteries—though of course he could charge them in sunlight in the morning—and closed his eyes. The silence and darkness pressed in around him, making him a little claustrophobic, but eventually he drifted off into a restless sleep.

When he woke, his body was aching. He decided to go gather more berries while he was still mobile. His broken bones and bruised and battered body would prevent him from doing too much crawling, and he needed to save his strength. He also needed to set his directional antenna up so his team could find him. It might be a long shot, but the batteries in his radio were fully charged and had a long standby life. His team was smart and would find a way to get here. All he had to do was give them every clue he could.

He gingerly made his way to the entrance. When he

reached the tube, he switched off his light again so it didn't give him away to anyone who might be looking. Not that the light helped much anyway. His eyes were so swollen they were nothing more than tiny slits on his painful and bumpy face. He could only imagine how crappy he looked right now.

When he made it out, a fresh breeze hit his face. It was cool and silent. There were stars here he'd never seen before; an entire galaxy shone in soft shades of pink, blue, and purple. He enjoyed the view for a moment before setting up his antenna under the berry bush, pointing it in the direction he'd come from, then gathered as many berries as he could, as quickly as he could, not wanting to be exposed any longer than he needed to be. He made his way back to his hiding spot, squashing some berries on the way.

Back in the enormous cavern, he switched his torch back on and set the berries close to his makeshift bed—soon he wouldn't be able to move without agony. His limbs were getting lighter and his pain increasing. What he wouldn't have given for a med kit, complete with painkillers. He set his radio as close to the entrance as he dared then tried to sleep—but every slight movement caused him so much pain that he whimpered involuntarily. He needed to be rescued, and soon.

He didn't know how long he could last, and as the hours drew out, he became more vividly aware of just how seriously hurt he was. It hadn't been so bad while he was being beaten—he'd focused on his hatred for the monster hurting him—and when he'd been given that foul stuff, he hadn't felt a thing. It had been blissful in an odd and slightly uncomfortable way. Now, though, he wanted to scream, but that would only make his pain worse, not to mention give away his hiding spot to the Huntowra.

P. Ryall

He bit down on a cry of agony when his limbs twitched involuntarily and tasted blood in his mouth. As he writhed, he forced himself to think of reasons to hang on, reasons to stay quiet when all he wanted was to scream like a squalling baby. Eventually, he could think a little clearer and that helped, but he dared not move again. Every few hours, he reached down with his less painful arm, picked up a few berries and shoved them into his mouth through tears and whimpers. Outside the tunnel entrance, there was a pinpoint of light.

It was daytime again.

Refugees

Chapter 28

Seth woke after what seemed like forever. His pain had numbed somewhat after these last few days, but he had all new pains. The kind you got from lying on a hard surface for days, and he was stiff from not being able to stretch out thanks to his injuries. He also desperately needed more berries. He would have to gather some, even if he had to bite down on something to keep himself from crying out. His face was still swollen, and he suspected he had internal bleeding as well. His belly was rounded and hard, like a balloon had blown up inside him. He didn't know exactly what that meant, but it wasn't normal. His arms and legs were definitely broken.

Seth tried again to roll over onto his tummy and made it as far as his side before he had to stop, drawing in ragged breaths and being careful not to jolt suddenly. Still focused on his breathing, he heaved himself into a crawling position.

He dragged himself to the entrance of the tunnel and peeked outside. The sun wasn't as hot as he'd expected it to be, but it was sure nice to get a look at it briefly. He carefully looked around him, making sure it was clear before leaving the mouth of the tunnel. He leopard-crawled to the berry bush and checked his directional antenna was still in position, clear of obstacles yet hidden under the brush where the Huntowra would hopefully not find it, or him.

His walkie crackled with static, but he clamped down on his instinctive flash of hope. There were many reasons the radios got static: sunspots and flares, for instance. Interference from other radios, something blocking the path of the antenna, so many other things. A couple more minutes of him picking the berries from the lowest branches went by quietly and then he heard it: a patchy voice muffled by the tunnel before it went quiet again. He turned as fast as he could in his current state and made his way back inside. He would try to get a message out. He just hoped he wasn't losing his mind.

Once back in his safe spot, he grabbed the radio. "This is Lieutenant Colonel Seth Adams. Can anyone hear me?"

He left it a minute then repeated his rank and name. He did this for about half an hour with no reply and was just about to give up when he heard a faint voice again.

"There's...trying to position...keep looking...east." It was breaking up, but he recognised Jye's voice.

"Jye," he yelled as loud as he could into his radio, "can you hear me? I'm here. I was hurt pretty bad but I'm somewhere the bastard can't get to me. I don't know where exactly. I went to the cliffs... Can you hear me, Jye?" He was nearly in tears he was so frustrated.

"Seth. Hell...breaking up again... I hear you but it's... Can you hear me, Seth?" Jye was still trying to get through.

Seth had to get out into the open. They were here now, so it was all or nothing. This was what he'd saved his energy for, to give himself every chance to go home again. He grabbed his stuff and heaved himself onto his belly again. Nausea rolled over him like a crashing wave and tiny lights popped in front of his eyes. He let out a bellow of agony then clenched his jaw shut—he would use the pain to help propel him outside again.

He pushed with his legs, ignoring the burning agony in his arms and ribs, and finally made his way to the entrance.

Refugees

There, he grabbed the directional antenna roughly, dragging it to his chest. He needed to get further out so they could hear him, so he crawled like a caterpillar as far as he could for as long as he could. He made it to the tree line after what seemed like hours. When he twisted the antenna, his radio started hissing again.

"Guys, I'm here. Can you hear me yet? I'm at the tree line in front of the cliffs."

He was so exhausted and hurt, he barely heard the response. "On my way. I hear you, Seth." Jye sounded panicked, but that didn't matter right now. All he cared about was getting home.

He just lay there. He couldn't go any further. Suddenly, the radio was filled with voices trying to find him, asking if he was okay, but he didn't have it in him to answer. He wanted to so badly, but he couldn't get his limbs to move again.

"Sorry, guys," he murmured before passing out.

* * * *

Jye was terrified. Seth had sounded terrible. He'd talked with the others this morning and asked if it would be worth lining up all the directional antennas towards the cliffs, as Hunter had predicted Seth would head for them. After some discussion, they'd decided there was nothing to lose by trying. They'd each taken up a section starting about three kilometres away from the base of the cliffs and roughly two kilometres apart so they didn't interfere with each other. He'd been talking to Hogan when he'd thought he heard another voice.

They needed to get to Seth now. He was hurt badly if he hadn't come out on his own. He radioed everyone else, and they converged on the area in front of Jye. It didn't take them long to get to the line of trees surrounding the cliffs, and they started fanning out to cover more ground. About ten minutes after they started looking, Ida screamed for help. She'd found him by some fallen trees.

Jye ran as fast as he could and was momentarily shocked when Travis came out of nowhere and ran straight past him. It had been a long time since anyone could outrun him; he sped up and skidded to a stop when he caught sight of his brother. He smacked right into Caleb without even seeing him there, muttered, "Sorry," under his breath, and then he was at Seth's side, stroking his hair and gasping in breaths between sobs.

Seth was scarily grey around the mouth and his head was bruised and misshapen. His eyes were swollen to slits, and his arms were splayed at weird angles. When Travis and Hunter rolled Seth gently, the whole side of his face that had been on the ground was bleeding as if it had been in a cheese grater. Several people gasped, and a couple actually threw up.

Jye let out an involuntary snarl and crouched low to the ground, his stripes flashing like a neon warning sign.

* * * *

Hunter looked sharply at him and shoved Travis and another man out of the way roughly. "Best you fellas get the hell back. The Talgra puppy's in protection mode right now."

Everyone stopped dead.

Travis must've been the only one who didn't realise what was happening, but sharp intakes of breath from everyone around him told him this wasn't the moment to push for an answer or to try to restrain Jye, even if it was to help Seth. He looked at them, at their horrified faces, and then it clicked.

Refugees

"Oh."

Of course, it made sense now. He'd heard about surrogating, it was the way Talgra adopted, and Jye had actually told him he considered Seth a brother. He should've known. They became murderous if their family or adopted family was threatened or hurt, even by accident. He'd never understood before, but now looking at Jye's expression and the obvious pain on his face, it was clear these adoptions weren't the same as they were on earth. Jye looked as though a piece of himself was shattered. As though he felt Seth's agony and his own on top of it.

Travis looked away suddenly, tears springing to his eyes and spilling down his cheeks quietly. He steadied himself for a minute, wiped his thumb across his nose then spoke. "If you need me to get anything, just say it, Jye. I won't do anything to threaten your brother, but I can't just stand here either. He's my best friend, and I love him too."

Jye looked at him then, tears streaming silently down his own cheeks, and nodded. "I know you do," he croaked then carefully picked Seth up. "We need to get him home. He needs a healer right now or he won't make it to nightfall."

They both nodded in agreement. "Well…we'll get a portal set up. Don't worry, Jye. Your brother will be home soon enough." For the first time in anyone's memory, Hunter was speaking gently.

Travis glanced at him. His eyes had softened and were shining with moisture. Clearly, he knew how deep this adoption thing was, and it moved him.

Hunter and Hogan opened the portal while the other team members stood guard. Travis stood as close to Jye as he could without getting snarled at, and Jye held Seth as though he were about to shatter, which he probably was.

"Right, everyone, it's time to go. We'll get most of you through first then Jye and Seth, followed by Travis, Hunter, and myself last," Hogan said firmly, all traces of his youth gone for the moment.

Everybody nodded quietly. Most looked at Seth and Jye before stepping through the portal.

When it came time for Jye to step through, he turned to Travis. "Can you come with me? I might need the extra hands, and I know you care as much about him as I do."

The look on his face shook Travis; he was almost pleading. "Of course. Just let me know what to do. I'm right here, okay?"

"Okay. Just grab his other side and we'll hold him"

Travis took the indicted side.

"Very carefully now. Then we walk him through, nice and slow."

The portal ride home was smoother than getting here had been, and there was no stinging sensation either. The surrounding room erupted into chaos and noise as soon as Hunter and Hogan came through. There were people everywhere, ogling them, clearly curious. Someone had obviously told them about the adoption.

Jye was lost in a panic, calling out for a healer, and didn't see all the curious eyes on him.

Chapter 29

Travis was wondering if he should let go of Seth but didn't have the nerve to ask Jye if that was okay. He'd just noticed Seth's hands. They were chained in front of him and his arms were as scratched up as his face. He made a sick choking sound in his throat, and Jye glared at him briefly before following Travis's gaze. Jye's breath hitched, and he swayed slightly. Travis adjusted his stance so if Jye fainted, he wouldn't drop Seth.

A small woman with blond hair in a loose braid pushed her way through the crowd. "Excuse me, please move." She shoved a few stubborn people aside regardless of the fact that they towered over her. "Oh, for the stars above, I'm needed urgently. Get out of my way." Her voice was strained but firm and clear until she gasped at the sight of Seth. "Oh no. Jye, I need you to lower him to the floor, please, and I'll need some space to work on him." She gave Jye a very stern look, and he nodded once.

He was gentle when he laid Seth on the floor, cradling his head. Travis stepped back when he was relieved of Seth's left side and watched helplessly as the blond healer kneeled next to him.

* * * *

Hannah quietly went to work, using her magix to help heal the man's injuries, but since he was human and had no magix of his own, there was a limit to what she could do for him. His many broken bones and the swelling and bruises were fairly standard, but the damage to his organs…she didn't know if she could do much for them. She would try, though, for Jye, who'd also be feeling his agony. It was a physical link between them, and he would always feel his surrogate's extreme emotions and illnesses or injuries as if they were his own, only dulled. It was strange that he'd surrogated a human, and she wasn't sure how that would impact the bond, but it seemed as strong as any she'd encountered. She looked up at Jye, her friend, and held his eyes, knowing he would understand.

* * * *

Hannah was doing everything she could, but Seth needed more, and Jye knew it.

"Crap. Travis…" Jye spun on his heel and almost collided with him. "Can you call your healing people and get them to come here? We can't move him anytime soon, but the ring will provide them with anything they need, equipment or medicine."

"On it." With that, Travis was gone, his phone at his ear.

He was back within ten minutes, with two paramedics and a field doctor who were recent additions to the A.S.U personnel. They were fully geared up, with a stretcher and first aid kits in hand.

"All right, let's have a look." The doctor sounded so kind, but it didn't stop Jye from wanting to rush to his brother's side. Instead, he locked his legs in place and balled his hands into fists while the doctor looked over Seth.

"Hmm, okay." He palpated Seth's abdomen and checked his eyes. "We have an operating theatre set up and prepped. This man needs surgery and a blood transfusion right now. I believe he's ruptured his spleen. Depending on the severity of the bleeding, we may need to remove the spleen altogether, but there's a chance we can repair any tears to the organ or the lining around the organ, which would mean he wouldn't need a splenectomy. He's lost a lot of blood, so the transfusion is essential either way. We have universal donor blood on hand and plasma if we need it. We'll also need to check for other internal injuries once we get the bleeding under control."

The paramedics lowered a stretcher and carefully shifted Seth onto it, strapping him in tightly.

"Right, let's get this man to theatre," the doctor announced and walked off, running his hands through his cropped hair.

Jye looked at Travis for a split second then darted off after the trio wheeling his brother away from him. He needed to know that Seth would be okay, so he would watch the surgery for himself from the view box that overlooked the theatre. It had started out as an interrogation room but was converted when the number of injured humans became high enough that they felt the need to employ medical personnel and create space for them to work effectively. Jye was grateful to the humans now for their insistence on having a theatre, hospital wing, and fully stocked pharmacy, though he'd initially thought they were just being silly. He would never again think that, and if anyone else, of any species, had a problem with the new facilities, he would stand and speak in their favour.

In the four hours that followed, Jye chewed his fingers and anxiously paced in front of the observation glass. His nerves felt like they were on fire and nothing could stop the burning.

His younger brother Ethan called in with some food and a cup of coffee. "Here ya go. Apparently worried people drink coffee to stay awake while waiting for news." He slid a glance to the window then back to his brother. "That was a different way to introduce our newest family member, Jye. You sure kept this quiet." He gave Jye a sharp look, clearly unhappy at being kept in the dark. "I think Mom's making him a blanket as a welcome."

Jye just nodded, ignoring the brash comments altogether, never taking his eyes off the window. After a minute, he found his voice. "This bond, it's a lot different to what I thought it would be. I'd heard it would be the same as with you guys, my own blood brothers, yet this feels much stronger. Maybe because he's just so fragile." His voice cracked on the last word and he shook his head, as if that would stop him from breaking down.

"Well, lemme know if there's anything I can do, okay?" Ethan clapped him on the shoulder, his eyes softened in sympathy, then turned, without another glance at the operation happening in front of him, and left.

No one else came in after that, but he could hear bustling and talking now and then, and he tensed every time. He didn't want anyone in here. This was a private matter, a family matter, and he was the only family Seth had here.

Finally, the surgery was complete, and they wheeled Seth into the hospital wing. As Jye accompanied the team, the doctor told him Seth was a real fighter and he was hopeful of a full recovery. He hadn't been able to save the spleen, though, so Seth would need to avoid getting sick as much as he could, and if he did, they'd need to start antibiotics straight away to prevent any complications. Jye listened with every fibre of his being. He would ensure that everyone knew that Seth needed to stay dry and warm on scouts, and if anyone was sick, they weren't allowed near him.

"Now, when we get him settled in, he'll still have these tubes and stuff attached to him. I placed Seth in an induced coma to let his body rest and heal. He was severely dehydrated, malnourished, and he lost a lot of blood. It's going to take time for his body to recover enough for us to wake him up. In the meantime, we'll monitor him closely. Sometimes people do have some bleeding after a splenectomy, but it generally settles quickly without further surgery. But if he's bleeding too much or fast then we'll need to intervene. But I'm sure Seth won't need that." He smiled so earnestly that Jye believed him.

Though he had lots of questions, he didn't ask any now. He just wanted the doctor to get his brother better and if that meant tubes and wires and stuff everywhere, so be it. He could ask the questions later, when Seth was awake and okay again.

After getting everything sorted with Seth, Jye went to find Travis to tell him everything he'd been told and thank him for these last few days. Jye had felt so lost and Travis had been an anchor keeping him grounded and focused. He doubted the man knew how comforting it was to feel that way with anyone other than his family, or how scared he was about these feelings he seemed to have towards Travis. He'd never noticed any feelings start to evolve; they'd taken him completely off guard and now he didn't know what to do. He was torn between just blurting it out or saying nothing yet.

He wandered the upper floor corridors until he got to the grand staircase where he suddenly felt exhausted. He sat on the top step and stared down into the large meeting room. People still buzzed about, but none of them saw him there and he was glad, because he just wanted to sit quietly for a minute. No questions or chatter. Travis's soft, clear voice broke the quiet moment, and Jye looked up to see the other man had changed into everyday wear.

Travis smiled and sat opposite him on the same step, and said nothing for a while, just shared the silence. When they did talk, it was mostly about Seth. Jye expressed his fear of all the equipment and then Travis expressed his disdain of the disinfectant smells that all hospitals seemed to have. It was a simple conversation, and exactly what he needed.

* * * *

After a while, they lapsed back into silence and listened instead to the chatter below them, which had turned to the annual ball preparations that would soon start. Apparently, the emperor knew how to throw a party. Jye told him that his daughter had always loved the balls, loved how everyone came dressed in their fanciest clothes and ate, danced, and made friends with people from all over the universe, and her father continued to honour that love.

As the excitement downstairs grew, he couldn't help wondering if any of them even knew that a life was hanging in the balance upstairs. That was unfair, though. They'd all lost their princess, and despite the sadness, they still kept living. That took real courage, to pick yourself up after a loss like theirs and keep on doing what was needed.

Travis's attention was drawn to the fairy queen. He'd always felt something a little off with her. Her actions and words were kind and beautiful, yet her body language suggested she didn't like this place, or anyone in it. She stood as far from the stairs as she could, near an archway that led to some lower levels, and recoiled a fraction when a young woman stood too

Refugees

close to her, her brows pulled together as though trying to control her temper. Yet she should've been almost totally relaxed with all the Starling Trumpets in this room.

"Hey, I know this probably sounds weird, but what's up with the fairy queen?" he couldn't help but ask Jye.

"What do you mean? She seems like her normal self to me." He shrugged. "She's always been a bit different. They say it's because she was infused with some Huntowra magix, which affected her a bit. The fairy portal won't let her in, you know, so it must be true. The only beings who can't go to the fairy world are the Huntowra. She's been trying desperately to go, though, to pay her respects to her people. She travels there every three months just to see if it will allow her entrance, but it never does. We send an escort with her because a Huntowra, one of the worst actually, had tried to get to her. Thankfully, our people arrived when they did, or there's no telling what would've happened to her."

"So, she goes there and what? Looks around or burns some herbs or something?" Travis wondered.

"No, she has a prayer ritual. She'll randomly pick up stuff and say an ancient prayer and then she returns home again."

This must've been common with the fairy folk, maybe a religious thing. He let it go and got up. "I'm gonna get some grub. You hungry?"

It was a simple question, but it took Jye a minute to answer him. "Sure. Okay."

Chapter 30

The next few weeks were hard for everyone. There was no lead about why the Huntowra had taken Seth, or what it had hoped to achieve. He'd been woken from his coma just a few days ago, and his recovery would still take some time, though Hannah had done well healing his lesser injuries.

"Damn, Jye, you look like your face got a makeover with mine. Did you go to the same beautician?" Seth had quipped when he'd first seen him.

Jye had snorted coffee out of his nose, which made both Seth and Travis laugh like little children.

They'd been sitting cross-legged on the bed playing a card game, and it looked like Seth was winning. He had a big stack of plastic discs in different colours, while Travis only had a few. Jye sighed a little and sat next to Travis at the foot of the bed, tucking a leg up under himself and settling in to watch the game. He felt more comfortable being protective now that Seth knew about the surrogating, and what it meant. He'd worried that the news would upset his new brother, but he'd just snorted and rolled his eyes.

"Don't be so daft. Why would it bother me? I count you as a brother too, you know." His tone implied that Jye should've known this fact already. He was chewing on a stack of sandwiches and speaking between mouthfuls. "Family isn't always blood. We silly humans tend to adopt people as family

Refugees

even without the paperwork or mystical bond stuff." He'd shrugged like it was no big deal.

Of course, it was a tremendous deal to a Talgra, but the way Seth had said it, it felt like Seth's way of adopting him. It was so odd that these humans had so many extremes, and that they could always surprise you. He'd never met a species like them before. He sat back and leaned on the little table behind him and watched his brother beat Travis soundly at cards.

* * * *

Travis had to pick a replacement for Seth while he was out of action, and he didn't want another human to get snatched on his watch, so he'd asked Peter. He didn't know him that well, but the guy seemed like he could take care of himself, and there had been a lot of rumours surrounding him. Part of Travis was just plain curious, but another part felt he was more lethal than he let on, even to his own family. He refused to fight, but if his back was up against a wall, Travis would bet he'd come out of it victorious. There was something in his face that just screamed dangerous, though he couldn't say what.

He'd originally thought of Ethan, Peter's twin, but he seemed too relaxed and nonchalant for Travis's peace of mind—his men and their safety were his absolute number one priority. He could've asked a healer or a dragon—Mirren would surely love to stretch his wings in his non-human form, but honestly Travis didn't feel ready to see the dragon in his original form just yet. He got along with the dragon, though Mirren was more formal and sometimes acted like he was a million years old—which, for all he knew, he could've been. He didn't really know much about dragons, and hadn't even realised at first that he'd actually met a few until the others explained.

"The sentient dragon species have two forms. The first is their natural, winged form, and the other was adopted centuries ago so they could blend in and interact with other species. So, now when they're outdoors, they're in their original form, and when they're in new places or where there's not much room, they use their other form, the human-looking one."

Travis had been stunned and noticed then that they all seemed to be albino, but without the pink eyes. Their eyes ranged from amber to green to blue, and they were always very bright, as though a light was shining inside them, and their hair was only ever a very pale blond.

So he'd chosen a Talgra and knew straightaway that he needed to have a Taylor on his team—everyone considered them the best, after all. Out of the thirteen brothers, Bryant was generally the first choice for missions, but he'd developed a reputation for being unreliable. He was too easily side-tracked and counted on everyone to be able to look after themselves, even the ones without magix. He liked that about Bryant because he didn't smother you like some did, but there were times you had to have your friends' backs, and he wanted someone there who would.

Jeff, Jye's twin brother, was an amazing warrior but could be too emotional. He felt his enemy's pain and sometimes hesitated—not a bad thing but it might lead them into a dangerous situation. Travis was still raw from what had happened with Seth. He needed to feel secure in who went with them now.

There were two sets of triplets, too, but he didn't know them all yet. Of these brothers he knew only two, Thackery and Theodore. Their third was away on a long and dangerous mission to gather intel and look for survivors with two older

Refugees

Taylor brothers, Knox and Dylan, who'd never set foot on earth. Thackery and Theodore were brilliant as a team but they were busy with another mission right now, clearing out the debris left after the most recent battles on their world, and they were starting to rebuild soon, so he didn't know how long it would be before they returned.

When he'd first thought of Peter, he almost dismissed him then remembered the time he'd seen him coming home from the Qualterra with Jeff, and a stray Shrogan had tried to follow them. He'd whipped a truly amazing sword from nowhere and cut the beast's arm clean off without even breaking a sweat. His whole being had changed in that moment, and a wave of something had seemed to come off Peter in every direction. Nobody else had noticed or felt anything, so it might've been his imagination. That was the kind of man Travis wanted for his team, so he'd sought out Peter. At first, he seemed ready to say no, and with such a pretty woman spending so much time with him, it was easy to guess why.

"Sorry, ma'am," Travis said when he'd walked in on their conversation.

She'd laughed at him then excused herself, saying something about needing to stretch anyway. Peter's gaze had stayed with her until she was no longer visible and then he'd sighed, seeming a little sad for her absence.

"I really am sorry for interrupting."

He nodded once, pursing his lips, which made him look annoyed. "Okay, what's up..." He frowned and shook his head in exasperation. "Ah crap, sorry. I can't remember your name."

"Travis. I need to ask you a favour." He breathed in then the words poured out in a rush. "Can you please be my team member until Seth gets well again? I know you prefer to stay away from the action and stuff, but it's only short term, like maybe a month." He threw him what he hoped was a pleading look.

Peter went very still and didn't answer, looking at the table. Had he even heard him?

"Of course the dummy will help you," came the high and weirdly wispy voice of his friend from behind them.

"*What*? You can't volunteer me for stuff, woman," he snapped at her, his voice an octave higher. He flushed bright red, crossed his arms over his chest in a huff, and stuck out his tongue. "I don't have to do anything if I don't wanna."

She just laughed at him, told him to stop being a baby about it, and help his friends and brother out. "Don't forget, Jye's adopted that poor man who was beaten almost to death. That makes him your brother too, doesn't it? Well, I mean sort of, anyway." She poked her tongue out at him and set down a plate of lasagne, before turning to Travis. "Don't worry, he gets grumpy when he's hungry, and he's peed off cause I've been able to translate more of his text than him."

"Hmph," Peter grumbled around a mouthful of food.

"He was going to offer to help anyway." She looked at Peter sternly. "Weren't you?"

"Mph, geah, I'b bas Cana," he mumbled. He swallowed, finally, and looked at Travis. "Yeah, okay. I'll do it, but only till Seth's better. I have other important things to do. Stabbing stuff isn't really my party." He made a sick little noise, and the woman placed her hand on his arm gently for a second.

"Thanks," he mumbled then left them to it.

Refugees

The first mission they were going on together was happening. In the next twenty-four hours, they'd be in the Qualterra and wouldn't be back for a week. Travis wanted to spend as much time visiting Seth as he could, so he'd grabbed the old poker set from home and they played poker the whole afternoon, even though he knew he'd get his butt handed to him. He didn't mind, though, because he got to see his best mate. Soon, he'd be gone, and going to the Qualterra was always a high-risk mission.

Jye would stay with Seth and make sure he was resting, exactly as the doctor had ordered. Travis smiled. Jye was a bear when it came to looking after Seth, who was really just a stubborn child demanding playtime. Seth had wanted to go back to work, but Jye had won the argument—only because Seth was still having trouble getting up without wincing. He'd tried, but when Jye had gently pushed him back into the pillows and he hadn't been able to stop it, he'd reluctantly agreed to stay put. For now.

The afternoon went by so fast, and when a nurse came in with a tray of food for Seth, Travis said his goodbyes and got up, stretching his arms out and rolling his head to loosen the stiff muscles. Jye didn't move. He was clearly staying here again, as he'd done since the day they'd come home carrying a badly beaten Seth between them. He kept inviting Jye for dinner to give him a break and get him out of the medical wing, and he'd accepted a couple of times, but he always came right back as soon as he'd eaten.

"Hey, guys," he said just before he left. "I'm heading out on a mission tomorrow, so I won't be able to call in until I get back. But I'll come see ya as soon as I do, okay?"

"Dude, you're going on a mission without me? That's

cold, man," Seth joked then he laughed and immediately winced. "Get outta here, ya boof-head. Be safe and see ya soon."

Travis smiled and nodded to them both. It seemed Seth was about to try to teach Jye how to play poker. He left them to it and went to grab some Chinese takeaway then headed home for a hot shower and an early night. But he struggled to get to sleep. This would be his first mission since Seth's abduction, and it played on his mind, but eventually he drifted off and didn't wake until his alarm screamed at him at six o'clock. He smashed the top of the alarm and unburied his head from the pillows. This would be a long week.

Refugees

Chapter 31

Peter had been torn between amusement and anger when Jayne volunteered him for missions. He'd wanted to be angry and yet he couldn't find it within him to do so. She was so infuriating, sometimes, and yet he kind of enjoyed it. He'd already decided he would volunteer, but it would've been nice to do it himself. Jayne had become such an important part of his world in the few short weeks he'd known her, even though it hadn't been easy getting used to her quirky dress sense or take-charge attitude. There was something she wasn't telling him about herself, but he wasn't pressuring her for answers. Yet. If they became any closer, he would. Hell, if they got any closer, they'd be dating, if he were being honest about it. He smiled and shook his head—if you'd asked him a month ago, he would've said there was no way possible he'd get that close to anyone. Yet here he was, and she'd just slipped right into his life and made herself at home.

Her little shop was opening tomorrow. She'd taken a couple of days off from translating to finish setting up. She had balloons and arches of little pinwheels to hand out to children, lolly sacks, and lucky door prizes for both the children and adults…and so much more, he couldn't even begin to remember it all. She'd convinced him and Jeff to help her staple and tape up fliers announcing her store's opening, and even sent ads out via email and placed them in the local newspapers. He could only imagine her satisfaction and pride. He knew her well enough now to know she was a perfectionist. Everything she did turned out perfectly, whether it was making food or translating languages, nothing was too hard for her.

He envied that. Even with all his magix, he couldn't do half as well as she did, so he'd started trying to learn from her. He took notes on how she recognised distinct patterns that showed the change of language in the texts, and he'd openly asked her to show him how to make some food so he could do it too. She was always kind and teased him a lot, which somehow didn't annoy him. It just felt right having her there, and it saddened him when she went home at the end of every day.

Spending those few days away from her had felt so bad, it was almost like he'd lost Lilah all over again. He should've felt panicked about that, but oddly didn't. She got along really well with Jeff too, and he seemed to miss her almost as much when she wasn't there. Ethan was curious about her but avoiding her after that first meeting. It had been really awkward, but he'd chosen not to tell her why in case she worried over it. Ethan had the potential to be her husband. His magix had called on him to take her hand and offer his then sent a spasm of electricity up his arm and into his chest, which was how marriage happened in their culture—except that no bonds appeared. He was a close match but not a perfect one for her.

Peter's relief had almost rivalled the sharp stab of panic he'd felt when Ethan had offered his hand. In that moment, he'd also felt the need to extend his hand to her, but he'd been denying himself for years out of grief so he didn't act on it. He didn't want to be married to a stranger. He and his twin had shared a look that clearly said they were both panicked and relieved for their own reasons. Jess was still upset that a human girl was more of a match for Ethan than she was. He'd never offered his hand to her after all the years they'd spent together.

Refugees

Watching Jayne move about amongst the books in his library was now his favourite pastime, and he looked forward to each day spent with her. There was no way of knowing what she would be up to at any given moment. She might be cooking, organising shelves, stacking books into mountains or any other number of things. The only thing for sure he knew for sure was that she would be dressed completely differently every single day. Everything about her outfit choices was random, except that she never had natural hair or eyes. Apparently she didn't like her own eyes or hair, but for some reason dying her hair wasn't an option. He hadn't asked why, but he was curious.

She was sitting amongst a fortress of books now, kneeling on the floor while looking through random books for fun. He suppressed a laugh and went to see if she wanted any help. She wouldn't, but he was looking for an excuse to be near her anyway.

She often said he walked like a panther, startling her, so now he clicked his fingers so she could hear him. "Hey, how's it going in there?" He smiled at her when she looked up. "You realise that I'm leaving tomorrow, right? And it's your fault. You volunteered me, so now you're gonna have to do all this work by yourself till I get back." He was mock scolding her, and she laughed, knowing he wasn't seriously upset.

"You're so funny. We both know you would've gone even if anyone hadn't asked you. That poor guy was so upset. He's really close to the guy who was hurt, and it happened when he was on a mission with him, right? I know I'd be freaked out. Not that I'd go anywhere other than here anyway. Not with…" She looked away for a moment.

It was there, whatever she wasn't telling him. She'd nearly said it without meaning to. He felt a stab of hurt. He didn't want her to keep stuff from him. She was a normal woman, so what could she possibly be hiding that was so bad she didn't want to talk about it?

After a minute, she recovered herself. "So, what time do you guys leave?" She gave him a forced, shaky smile.

"Oh…well, I think we leave around ten. It depends on whether there's any incoming personnel. I'll be ready and waiting by nine, but there's nearly always someone running late." He sat down next to her in the book fortress and looked around.

The book she was holding was a children's story about a dragon who found a boy and became friends with him.

"Wow, you really like that book, don't you?" She'd looked at his book and its pictures several times now.

"What? Oh, yeah. I don't know why, but it feels kind of familiar. Like I've read it before or something. I don't know, it's probably my imagination going bonkers, or maybe I've read so many books one of them is similar." She scratched her nose unconsciously and went back to fidgeting with the book edges, running her fingertips across the pages and drawing circles over the raised cover image: a Great One. He was so old he looked like he was a ghost with liquid gold eyes.

He was struck by an idea. "Did you know that the dragon is supposed to be Mirren's dad? His name is Meirden. He's the king of dragons, but he doesn't like to be called that. He's supposedly the oldest and wisest of all the dragons, and he's well over a thousand years old. I have another copy of this book. Would you like to keep this one?"

Jayne drew in a shocked breath and nodded enthusiastically. "Wow, really? Thank you. So, do Mirren and

Refugees

his dad talk much?"

"No, unfortunately he was sealed away somewhere, and we haven't been able to find him, or the other Great Ones, for that matter. That's one reason we go into the Qualterra. Apparently, the doorway to wherever they are is there. We're trying to find it so we can get their help. Nobody really knows if they're even okay, but we have to try." He stared off for a bit. What were the chances the Great Ones *were* still alive? And had the netherworld ever been in the Qualterra at all?

There were other reasons to go there, though. The Huntowra seemed to avoid it as much as possible, so maybe the reason was something worth finding. A weapon, perhaps, or some powerful magix that hadn't been seen before. Anything was better than nothing.

"Well, I'm bushed. I'm gonna take my new book and head home. I hope you have a safe trip," she added as she stood up, and he smiled at her choice of words. If only she knew what it was like there...but he was glad she didn't.

Peter had a long, hot bath to unwind from the day. It hadn't been stressful, but he was as exhausted as if he'd run a marathon. He would miss what his brothers referred to as a boring life while he was away, so he was enjoying his last night at home. He hated going to the Qualterra, so he let his mind wander over today. He'd started taking Jayne for walks to the coffee shop. She was a slow walker, in part because of those crazy shoes she always wore, but she also seemed to tire so easily. Still, she seemed to enjoy walking as much as he did.

He'd discovered they had a lot of things in common on their walks. He hadn't been able to stop himself from asking her about her likes and dislikes, things she enjoyed, and what her goals were for the future. She said she listened to all different bands but her all-time favourite was Roxette. He'd loved all the songs he'd heard from them, but his favourite band was Skillet. They had a darker edge to their music that he just enjoyed listening to, and he could tell by the way they sang them that the lyrics had meaning. Jayne was also a big coffee lover but for some reason limited herself to only two cups a day. When he asked her why, she went quiet and shrugged. Her favourite food was sushi. Peter had admitted he hadn't tried that yet, but it sounded interesting. Apparently, he would either love or hate it. There was no real in-between when it came to sushi. Jayne's favourite colour depended on her mood, while he'd always loved greens, and always would. Lilah had had the most beautiful green eyes.

He'd thought it would upset Jayne to hear that, but she'd only reached out to take his arm lightly and hold onto it. He understood that this was her way of offering him comfort, and it had become a familiar trait in the weeks following. If he was upset or sad, she instinctively reached out for him and lightly touched his arm, and the second he felt it, his body would relax. It had scared him how intuitive she was at first, but now he didn't even give it a second thought.

His feet were bobbing away in the water when he realised he'd been in the bath for much longer than he'd planned on, and his toes looked like wrinkled-up stubs. He used his toe to snag the plug chain and pull it from the water, reluctant to get out. He was so tired that when he fell into bed, he was asleep before he even finished yawning.

Chapter 32

Travis, Ida, Tess, Caleb, and Peter were waiting for the last two members of their team. This was a week-long trip into Qualterra and everyone was nervous. They had to have someone, or a few someones, who could use magix in case of an attack from the Shrogan. Caleb and Tess had already scouted their camping site, and Ida was the tech expert who'd take professional quality photos of the newly found ruins at the top of a megalithic staircase. The A.S.U had randomly picked the other two members. Nobody knew who they were yet, only that they were backup. The brass liked keeping the numbers in teams at seven—four if it was a special ops mission, but Travis hadn't had enough training to go on those.

He huffed out a breath and fidgeted with his gear, trying to ignore the chatter. He was nervous as hell, and though he'd slept okay, he still felt tired. He was used to working with Caleb and Tess, and Ida was familiar from a few missions. She was focused and scary smart, , and he was surprised at how well she fit in. Still, he missed Seth already, and they hadn't even left yet. Having Peter here kind of made up for that, and he was excited to see him out on a mission. He looked over at Peter now, surprised to see him chatting animatedly with Ida. Apparently, they were friends. He shifted his gaze to the familiar bickering between Caleb and Tess then sat on his sleeping bag and placed his head in his hands.

"You look like you're gonna barf." Caleb snickered at Tess while miming her being sick.

"The only one here who's gonna barf is you, you idiot, right after I punch you in your belly. Stop being such a jerk all the time." She waved a fist in the air to emphasise her threat.

Caleb chortled loudly, clearly not having been scared into good behaviour. They continued to spar with each other as though they were alone.

This would be a long week.

The sound of footsteps came from upstairs, and he jumped up and grabbed his bag from under him. He looked up then and paused. Hannah and Emmaline were dressed for travelling, making their way downstairs with bags. They were his backup? He blinked stupidly before recovering himself. He'd known them both for a couple of years now, but he'd never seen them to go into Qualterra.

Emmaline was a florist in her spare time. She was also a royal and a self-confessed moody bitch who apparently hated everyone. Jye had told him she'd been traumatised when a Huntowra murdered her cousin. He shuddered, because he now knew first-hand how brutal and sadistic the Huntowra could be. His heart ached for a second at the thought of the child, practically a baby, being tortured like Seth. No wonder Emmaline was this way. He'd never be the same after what had happened to Seth.

Hannah was a sweetheart, angelic and kind. She was half Visper, half Talgra and something of a prodigy. Her Visper traits were strongest, and he couldn't help wondering if her warrior side even existed. She seemed so gentle, he just couldn't picture her fighting.

He clapped his hands to clear his head and get everyone's attention. "Okay, let's do this. I'm not too worried

Refugees

about introductions right this second. Let's just get there and set up. We'll have an entire week to get to know each other when we're there."

He gestured for them to all gather, and Tess opened the portal. Travis took a deep and steadying breath then when almost all his team was through, he stepped through the portal and into Qualterra. Peter silently came through behind him and waved his hand to close the portal. Huh, that was different. Usually there was an incantation or at least some concentration, but not for Peter. Cool. He shrugged, and they set off towards the stairs.

After two hours of walking, they reached a ravine that meant they were close. Cliffs had sprung up all around them with little caves dotting them, though the ones up high were empty.

"Hey, did anyone else notice the higher caves are empty?" he asked no one in particular.

"Yeah, the Shrogan don't like heights," Tess said sarcastically, and Caleb snorted with laughter.

"Actually, the Shrogan don't use them during the warmer months because the cliffs are too hot. The lower caves are always shaded and a lot of them have little streams of fresh water running through them. When winter comes, they move up to the warmer and drier caves, where flooding and cold aren't an issue," Emmaline said, which was probably the most she'd said to anyone. And that was one thought he wouldn't repeat.

"Oh, that's so clever. They're still scary, though," Hannah quietly added, looking all around her.

They stayed close together on the walk, winding through the now-high cliffs and further into the Qualterra. The chatter was fairly friendly, though mostly the girls talked while Travis and Peter walked in silence. Peter had a serious look on his face, one Travis recognised. His dad had worn it when he had to go to the hospital for the first time after his friend passed away. It had gutted him to go back there, but his niece had needed surgery and her parents were travelling for work, so he and his dad had to take care of her when she'd fallen over in dance class and snapped her leg. He looked at Peter. Who had he lost here? He didn't know that much about him, just that he was a loner and definitely hiding stuff from everyone.

They finally reached the area where they would set up camp. There were enough empty caves to hide inside if a storm sprang up out of nowhere, as they sometimes did at this time of year. This was the last trip into the Qualterra before the storm season started for real, which meant that the threat of a Huntowra attack would lower significantly, though not completely. The Shrogan made up for that, though, seeming to get pepped up by the storms, but they were fairly easy to avoid when you were used to their patterns. Being extra peppy also meant they were less coordinated. They tended to fall over each other and start fights at the smallest provocations.

Peter was still silent. He stared off into space and sat like a rock for about three hours solid then sprang into action at the loud shrieking sounds coming from a nearby herd of Shrogan. It sounded like they were fighting each other, bellowing in agony and roaring like lions did when they were being territorial during mating season. When he realised they were quite safe, Peter sat back down, still lost in his own thoughts.

"Wow, you're a jumpy one today," Caleb said sarcastically to Peter.

Refugees

"Shut your mouth or I'll shut it for you," Emmaline exploded at him. She was wild with anger, her eyes narrowed, and her hair standing up like an angry cat's.

"Hey now, what's going on here?" Travis asked, looking at each of them.

"He'd better shut his mouth," Emmaline repeated with a hiss, glaring at Caleb, who sat there looking like someone had slapped him.

"Sheesh, what's your damn drama, chick?" he demanded at the same time Peter said, "Lilah died here."

Everyone went still and silent.

"They abducted her from Meakra, brought her here, and murdered her. It was the Elite Five, an assassin squad. They're worse than all the other Huntowra, except for the queens themselves. So, the reason I'm not so happy to be here and the reason Emma is pissed at you," he glared at Caleb, "is because her cousin, who was more like a sister to her, was murdered here. And she was my world. They took her from me, and she was only five." His voice cracked as the words rushed out, but he couldn't stop them.

Emma sat as still as a stone and stared at the ground with tears streaking her face. He wanted to reach out to her, but he was paralysed by pain.

"Oh crap. Shit, man… I…just, wow. I'm sorry, dude, I never knew," Caleb sputtered, trying to get the words out ."Gee, chick, sorry I was a dick. Guess if it was my little sis I'd be pretty messed up too." He nodded lamely at her in apology.

"She was more than our kin, she was also the heiress to our world, a princess, and the most powerful being who's ever existed," Jess quietly informed them all. "When she was a baby—we call them younglings—the elders placed her into the magix ring for a special power reading because some weird things kept happening around her. The ring sent her over to the Kalix ring, which lit up, sang her a lullaby, caused an earthquake, and created a whole new symbol, just for her. The light that emanated from her that night, with over ninety percent of her magix suppressed, was so powerful that it lit the entire village right up to the castle that was over six kilometres away. I was supposed to be asleep when my room lit up so bright I was sure it was daytime." She recounted this memory as though it were the happiest and most amazing thing to have ever happened. "That's how powerful she was, and why the Huntowra assassinated her. If she'd reached adulthood, she would've gained total control over her abilities and they would never have had a chance to win this war. So, her death was really the starting bell. Emma was with her when they came. She tried her best to stop them and then to get help, but it was too late. Peter was betrothed to her, and more than that, they share an eternal bracelet. That's why he wears a power band on his left arm. It's wrapped around the bracelet and helps to stop the pain caused by them being separated, which apparently includes death." She pointed to Peter's left arm.

* * * *

He raised it and let the band shimmer. The pain was ever-present and debilitating. Oddly, though, now that he thought about it, it hadn't been hurting at all lately. Not until now, anyway. He frowned then focused on the conversation again.

"So, if the princess had lived, we would all be safe now?" Ida asked sadly. "They're monsters. I mean, I knew that,

Refugees

but it never occurred to me they'd just kill a little kid. It just seems so...well, just so evil." She crossed her arms over her chest as though she were cold and shivered.

"The bastards! Killing little kids is just too far. I wanna kill as many as I can for her and all the other kids they killed." Caleb was nearly in tears, fury lacing his words.

Peter's heart thumped with gratitude for his kindness and sorrow for not particularly liking the man and his brash manner.

"The Huntowra don't view children as either defenceless or weak. Their special ability is sensing power, even when it's hidden. They sent the most powerful warriors to assassinate Lilah, which had three main effects. The first," Peter held his finger up to illustrate his point, "was to warn any others who would fight. They wanted to stop the Talgra and Whistler from going to the aid of the Aggaron. Then, it was common knowledge that Lilah was special, the precious one, and betrothed to me, which involved the Talgra, so both her world and mine were looking for her, distracted... We all looked for years. Nobody knew the Huntowra were plotting to wipe out the Aggaron as well. They'd already started preparing before they sent the Five to kill Lilah. And last, it got her out of the way. She was still so young and had many power bands on her, so she had no ability to protect herself even if she'd known how to." He looked at each face and saw his own thoughts mirrored on theirs.

This was way more organised than they'd thought the Huntowra capable of. Their leaders were content thinking they knew the enemy, but they'd failed to see the blindingly obvious. They either had a leader who was more intelligent than the Huntowra they'd seen or they were working for someone who hadn't shown themselves yet.

The group spent the rest of the night talking about the Huntowra and who could be leading them. It was clear they had a boss, but whoever or whatever it was, they didn't know.

They slept fairly well for a few hours until a horde of Shrogan came stampeding by just before dawn. Their faces were flat, squashed like a bulldog's, but nowhere near as cute, and they were all bald, though a few had tufts of hair here and there. Their ears were pointed at the tips but seemed unremarkable other than that, and they had strong, muscular bodies, which were only covered with something like loin cloths. Some had necklaces, and they all had arm bands and weapons. They crashed into each other and the cliffs either side of the ravine but paid no attention to the group huddled inside the barrier. Something must've spooked them or riled them up.

"That's really odd. They never ignore us," Tess said in a worried tone, mirroring Travis's thoughts.

"What were they running towards?" asked Caleb.

"Actually, I think they're running away from something," Jess added.

"Okay, what the hell can make them run away? Aren't they, like, immortal and fearless or something?"

"Behemoths and large numbers of Huntowra are pretty much all we've seen them run from. Oh, and the Great Ones. Well, Mirren...but technically he's a Great One so, you know..." Emma shrugged. "They flee real fast from them." She motioned with her hands and chewed on a protein bar.

They all stared after the Shrogan, too shocked to do much else.

Refugees

It was Travis who broke the silence. "Hey, let's get this gear packed up. We'll move camp to the ruins. That way we're out of the way of stampedes…and, you know, the foulest smell ever." He wrinkled his nose and waved a hand in front of his face. The stench really was that bad.

Peter chuckled quietly and rolled up his sleeping bag. He never needed it, but it was softer than the ground had been. He felt a little better this morning. It seemed that by talking about Lilah last night, he'd somehow lessened his hurt, and he was grateful for it. His arm was starting to really burn now, though, but he wouldn't say anything. The burn was normal, but it seemed worse than he could ever remember it, and that worried him. He needed to have a chat with Matt. Maybe he needed a second power band.

Chapter 33

Emma hated scouting trips. She hated being around people in general and wanted to get back to her training sessions. She'd done all she could on her own, though, so now she needed to enlist the help of the only Great One she knew, Mirren. They had training techniques lost to most other species, and she wanted desperately to learn as much as she could. His knowledge would be limited as he was still young by dragon standards, but it was better than nothing at all. She just hadn't yet figured out how she would do that or get him to keep quiet about it.

She'd found her warrior armour when the monsters took Lilah, and she'd kept that information a secret from everyone. She wasn't ready to let them know she would fight with them shoulder to shoulder in this war. She would protect her loved ones, and Lilah's 'dear ones,' as she used to call them. She did this for her, for the sweetness and innocence that had been lost and for all who'd suffered at the merciless Huntowra's hands.

She glanced a few times at Peter. He was so sad here it made her want to rage and lash out, but she took some deep breaths and steeled herself to remain quiet and reserved, as a proper lady and royal should. Come battle time, though, she would be on the front line and nobody would get her to stand down. This was personal, and every single life here depended on them all working and fighting together.

Peter's revelations to the group last night had her thinking. If the Huntowra had a boss and they weren't just randomly attacking, that meant all their attacks had the potential to be ambushes. But if that were really the case, how did they know where to lie in wait? As they made their way up the enormous staircase, she almost fell behind she was so lost in thought.

"Hey." Caleb looked unsure and avoided her gaze when she looked at him. "Um, I really am sorry. For yesterday, I mean. My baby sis is my world, if anything ever happened to her, I don't think I'd survive it. Anyway," he shrugged and for once, he was completely serious, "I was thinking, you know, about those Huntowra." He was speaking loud enough that everyone could hear him, and they were all paying attention. "So, you're, like, the only person to ever get away from them, and you know what they look like and stuff."

"What's your point?" she snapped coldly.

"Well, I'm a pretty good artist. My folks made me go to art school during the holidays, so, well, if you could describe them, I could draw them. Then we'd all know what the Five look like, and maybe it will help." He shrugged, and his cheeks reddened.

* * * *

Peter sucked in a sharp breath and blinked rapidly. Having an image of the Five would be helpful. He'd know who to go after first. He shot Emma a look, knowing instinctively that she was thinking the same thing. He frowned at her, and she dropped her gaze and pretended to fix her bag strap.

Peter had been taken by surprise yet again. First, Jayne had figured out how to remove the Huntowra's advantage, and now this. It wouldn't stop the Five, but perhaps it would give people a chance to escape before getting seriously hurt, and although he didn't like the man, Caleb was right. Emma was the only known being to survive a direct attack from the Elite Five. She'd been so close she'd reached out and hit them, and yet they'd let her live. He hadn't thought of this before now, but no one else had ever been in the sights of the Five and could still talk about it. Whether it was by accident or fate, they had someone who'd seen them up close and could describe them.

"Emma—"

"I know, Peter," she said. "Let it go, okay? I'll think about it." She shuddered.

They finally reached the top of the stairs, and Peter stopped to stare open-mouthed. It opened onto a large platform with columns spaced throughout, reaching up to a ceiling that stood some fifty feet high. Each one was covered with etchings—glyphs, Jayne had called them. This was a language, and the pictures represented words or phrases that, in certain orders, told stories or histories. There had to be hundreds of glyphs on each column, and if he started at the wrong one, it would change the whole meaning of the story. Jayne had shown him exactly how this could happen using the Egyptian hieroglyphs, so he'd have to be careful and find the correct starting point.

"I'll need to take photos of every single glyph here to study them and be sure I'm translating them correctly. And, if necessary, I have a genius language expert on call." He smirked and shook his head.

Jayne was a character, for sure, but she was brilliant and knew her way around languages. The translations they were working on had come a fair way, further than he'd managed on his own, but it was still far from being deciphered fully. There were parts that just didn't seem to fit, as though someone had

Refugees

added them afterwards, and yet there was no logical reason to do so.

He wandered around the columns slowly, trying to spot a possible starting point even though he didn't really know what to look for. Jayne would've known. It was too bad civilians weren't allowed, or he'd have insisted she come and see this place for herself.

In fact, he had asked if she could be granted access as an independent contractor, and the higher ups had agreed. They would discuss it then decide whether or not she would be invited along on these kinds of scouting trips. The thought of the quirky Jayne in all her crazy clothes here, in this world of decay and death, made him smile.

"What the hell are you smiling about?" Jess demanded. She'd snuck up on him.

"Oh...ah, nothing much, really. I'm just kind of surprised we didn't find this place years ago. It's like it was hidden or something, but I sort of remember this area from when I was a kid. It's really close to where I was hiding out. I guess I must've just been terrified or something." He shrugged, pretending that was all that had been on his mind.

In truth, he didn't want to talk to Jess about Jayne. Her hatred made him angry, and that wasn't the best thing. Jess felt betrayed and unwanted; she'd made that clear after they'd said goodbye to Jayne and Damian. Jess had screamed at Ethan in fury, and Peter had worried that this would upset his brother, who genuinely loved Jess though he'd never felt the powerful connection needed for bonding. Ethan hadn't been hurt, though. He'd just accepted that this was the way of it, as it had always been, and shrugged off the idea that he very well could've been bonded right now, and to a total stranger. That in itself was odd.

Generally speaking, the bonding only happened with those who were known to each other, yet none of them had met Jayne before.

"She seems familiar to me. Not really sure why, but there was a second there when I thought I knew her, you know?" Ethan had said to Peter, and although he wanted to dismiss it, he'd felt the same way.

She resembled Jess—and even Emma, if he were being truthful—but there were thousands of people who shared similarities in the universe, and nobody else seemed to notice. Of course, with all her costumes, she could really look like anyone from any world. Her skills were incredible.

Jess looked at him sourly and huffed, just as Ida sidled up beside them, making them both jump when she boomed, "Whatcha doing over here?" She'd clearly meant to interrupt them, and Peter was grateful for it.

He gave her a genuine smile and winked, which she returned.

Peter really liked Ida. She was a slight female, but fought better than most men he knew. She'd been a close friend since his return from Qualterra the first time. Back then, she was just a frail little thing with a broken heart. Her parents had died in a fire on some distant world, and she'd been left to fend for herself. She'd chosen the warriors' life, and even though she wasn't a Talgra, she'd been taken in and trained as one.

Her species was known as the Zamp. They were an obscure and tiny settlement of humanoids, small—averaging five feet in height—with ever-so-slightly pointed ears. Damian had called her an elf with vampire fangs. It had taken Peter months—and Damian showing them his favourite elf and

Refugees

vampire movies—to understand the context enough to find his teasing funny.

Ida had made friends with the people on Earth rather easily, and she loved to joke around with everyone. "So, what did I just break up there with Miss Prim-and-Proper?" Ida quipped, throwing a sideways glance at Jess then turning back to face Peter.

Peter chuckled and raised an eyebrow at her. "She's still annoyed that Ethan nearly got hitched to a lesser mortal." He snickered, knowing she would love hearing him use a mortal phrase like that, and she threw her head back and laughed.

Jess glowered at them from the other side of the ruins. It was nearly as big as two football fields and perfectly square.

Peter shook his head in dismay. "Shoot, Ida, why did you do that? You know how sensitive she is about stuff." He was almost grumbling, but his smile gave him away. He wasn't mad at her, not really.

"Well, you know what? The little 'princess,'" she used air quotes to show what she thought of Jess, "can get the hell over herself for once. Em's a princess too, and she doesn't carry on like a howling Shrogan, does she? Unlike Jess, Em doesn't have a giant stick up her—"

"Don't you dare finish that sentence, or I'll throw you over the edge, you nasty little imp," Jess thundered. She'd made her way round while Peter and Ida were wandering, taking pictures.

"Whatever...princess." Ida snickered, throwing her arms out like she was gesturing at the whole room, or mock bowing, causing Jess to flush and stalk off. She kept her back turned to the rest of the group and ignored anyone who spoke to her for the rest of the day.

* * * *

Travis had known this week would be a lengthy one, but if today was anything to go by, he'd seriously underestimated it. Jess was angry at everyone. Caleb was as obnoxious as ever. Tess was always sparring with him, which was really annoying. Emma was brooding. Ida was a real prankster, who kept cracking jokes at everyone, trying to make them all laugh.

The only one he didn't have a handle on yet was Hannah. She sat unobtrusively and watched the others with interest, as though assessing them all. She rarely joined in the discussions and never let herself get drawn into what inevitably turned into arguments. Travis wondered again how she would fare if she were to be drawn into a fight. Could she really take care of herself or would he need to protect her? Should he talk to her and let her know he would look out for her if she needed it?

A strange sound came from the flat land across from them. He'd been sitting separately from the group, who were all huddled by the campfire they'd made next to a giant panel that seemed to be some kind of oversized tablet, and there'd been a definite thunk. He supposed it could've been a Shrogan, but they generally roared or made other weird noises. This was something else. It went completely silent for a while then he heard it again, followed by some rustling. Travis jumped up and started scanning automatically, and again the sounds stopped.

"Caleb, Peter," he called.

They both looked at him curiously.

"Can I grab your help for a minute, guys?" He turned back to the edge, knowing they would obey.

Refugees

"S'up?" Caleb greeted him.

Peter stood with his arms crossed as though this were a normal thing to do, but his eyes were sharp.

"I heard a noise, thought it was a fluke cause it went real quiet but then I heard it again. It stopped as soon as I stood up. We might have company, guys. Be ready, okay? Don't want any more of my guys getting tortured…or dead." He looked directly at Peter.

* * * *

Peter nodded once. This was why he was here. Travis was shaken by what had happened to Seth under his command. Jye had asked Peter to come on this trip, worried about Travis, so Peter had agreed. Of course, he'd left the asking to Travis, though. The set up in the library and been for Travis's benefit. Jayne had cinched the deal by volunteering him, and he wondered if she'd known what was really happening.

"I'll take the shift while you all get some rest. Talgra don't actually need sleep so it's fine."

"I'm staying up with you. This is my unit. I need to do my bit too," Travis said sharply.

"Cool… I'll get teams of two organised for the other shifts and we'll rotate while we're here. That cool with you, boss?" Caleb waited for Travis to reply, seeming eager to be helpful.

Travis nodded, and Caleb went straight to the others and started organising the pairings, making sure not to put Jess with Ida or Emma. He'd obviously been paying attention. Then he sat next to Emma and spoke quietly. He was still being extra nice to her, and she nodded at something he said and gave him a rueful smile.

Peter watched Travis closely, not leaving his side. Then from behind him, he heard it too, a thunk sound followed by rustling. Wings.

"I think you're right, friend. The stampede this morning, the strange emptiness in the valleys, the sounds now... We're being watched, maybe even followed." He gestured for Travis to remain quiet. "Stay calm. If they see us react, they'll know we are onto them for sure. They might still think we were just organising a normal patrol before, but anything more obvious and we could be in trouble, depending on who's watching us." Peter's voice stayed quiet, and he was facing away from the ledge.

Travis looked out over it again and murmured, "Mm-hmm." After a minute, he made his way to the group and casually sat between Ida and Emma, and Jess hopped up and took the first shift with Peter.

"Gee, that's an ugly-ass creeper," Caleb announced a couple of hours later. He'd drawn the sketches of the Elite Five with Emma correcting him as needed.

Emma nodded and let out a tiny laugh. "Yeah, they were pretty gross."

Travis was curious. He wanted to see them, but before he could do anything, Jess let out a shriek, which was answered with a mocking laugh. Bryant made his way up the last few stairs, and Peter let out a huff.

* * * *

"Oi, what's that about then?" Bryant demanded.

"What the hell are you doing here, idiot? You're not

Refugees

supposed to be here," Peter shot back at him coldly.

"Brr. Gee, bro, get over it. They sent me to replace your sorry butt. You're needed back at A.S.U." Bryant shrugged as though this was obvious. Big brothers were such pains in the ass sometimes.

"What the hell do they need me for?" He was genuinely confused, and it derailed some of his anger at his older brother.

"No idea. Mom said to tell you to get your tail back and don't dawdle." He rolled his eyes. "Momma's boy," he added snidely.

Peter ignored the barb and turned to gather his stuff. Getting to go home was fine with him, but he was concerned about why he was needed. Nobody had ever needed him badly enough to send a replacement for him before. His speciality was staying out of the way and reading. That was it. A thought struck him, and he panicked. What if the rest of the passages had been translated?

He said some hasty goodbyes and made his way to a clearing where he could portal home. It took no effort for him, though he didn't show anyone else that. It was getting harder to hide his differences from his loved ones, and they wouldn't know what to do about him if they knew.

* * * *

Emma caught up to him just as he was about to open a portal, something he shouldn't have been able to do, and called out to him. "Wait, Peter." She walked forwards when he turned and looked at her questioningly. "Something's bothering me, and I wanna talk about it." She held up a hand to stop him from cutting her off, but seemed strangely shy. She crossed her arms over her chest and rocked from side to side then flicked her hair back with a tilt of her head. "I've been doing some thinking about what you said the other night, and I'm really worried. Like, my gut's gonna knot so tightly I'll split open worried. Peter, they know where to wait for us. They know where we are, and they're always there. Always." She frowned at him, hoping he'd understand.

"Yes, I've been thinking the same thing, actually. But without evidence, we can't just go around and tell everyone there might be a spy among us." He gave her a very stern look, clearly telling her to keep this to herself. "We need to trust one another. We'll find out who the traitor is and deal with it, but for now, just play along and don't give anyone any ideas that could lead them to the same conclusion. Whoever's working with the Huntowra is committing treason, and we know they have some sort of boss now, so let's just stay quiet and focused. They'll oust themselves soon enough." He smiled bleakly.

She nodded once, took a deep breath, then turned and left.

Chapter 34

Mirren was waiting for Peter. He seemed excited and bounced on his feet.

"Hey, what's going on?" Peter asked casually.

Nobody else was around so the waved his hand absently and the portal closed behind him. Mirren looked at him with curiosity but said nothing; he knew about Peter's extra special abilities and that he wasn't ready to talk about it yet.

"I don't know, actually. I just heard you were sent home and decided to come say hello." He smiled warmly and clapped his hands softly then shook them, something he often did when he was feeling particularly excited.

Peter eyed his hands warily for a moment. "So, what's got you all hyped up then? And who sent for me, and why aren't they waiting for me?" He was confused, but before his thoughts got too out of hand, Mirren let out an excited babble of laughter.

"I'm allowed to go out to this world now. Not to stretch my wings," he shifted uncomfortably, "but I'm allowed to explore and go to shops and the movies." His voice climbed in pitch on the last word and he was talking so fast he had to stop and suck in some air. He'd forgotten to breathe. "Oh, and Angel too. We've both been looking forward to this. The suit people from here said we had to 'prove' we could contain our wings before being allowed out. Isn't that great?" He looked at Peter with such excitement that he laughed.

"Well, congratulations. That's really cool. You're gonna love the little shops. Some friendly advice, though. If you go to a movie, you should take a light jacket with you. The theatres get cold for some reason." He winked.

Mirren blinked and nodded, taking his advice seriously, and murmured, "Thanks," just as the doors opened and Mathew strode in.

"Ah good, you're here. I needed your help. I asked Jye, but he's so busy looking after Seth, so I sent Bryant to get you." He stopped in front of them and sighed. Being an emperor suited him, but it looked as though he didn't get a lot of sleep nowadays.

"What's wrong?" Peter asked him solemnly. Was this Lilah related?

"What? Oh…nothing, really. I just hate setting up these balls by myself." He gestured around him, swinging his arms and turning in a full circle. "This is the first proper one we've had since the war forced us out of our homes, and I don't want it to be a disaster." He looked sharply at Mirren, who gave him a sour look in return.

He'd accidentally trodden on some poor soul in his dragon form. The man hadn't been seriously hurt and had laughed about it after he'd been healed, but Mirren wouldn't be allowed at the ball in his other form.

"So the girls are handling the layout for the floor and the foods, but I wanted to get your thoughts on the theme. We did dragon land," he threw another look at Mirren, who flushed bright pink, "and we've done the traditional themes from many worlds, but now, here we are, refugees on this new world and they have so many cultures and customs, I thought it'd be nice

Refugees

to honour them by incorporating their themes, maybe." He sounded unsure.

"Oh, yeah, um, okay. I know little about the balls here, but I think I know someone who can help. You don't mind if I ask Damian's sister to help me out, right?"

"Hey, that's a splendid idea. I'll leave it with you then. Don't forget to add her to the guest list either, and Damian too. I meant to add them the other day, but things were just hectic, and they've both been so helpful and kind to our people, unlike some." He turned on his heel and strode back out.

Did he realise he did that or was it just something that happened when you became an emperor? He let out a low chuckle.

"Why is it funny?" Mirren asked him innocently.

"It isn't. I was thinking of something else."

Mirren shrugged then wandered off, muttering under his breath, which left Peter standing there alone.

Seriously, they'd dragged him home for this? He arched an eyebrow and shook his head. Typical Matt. Parties seemed to be the only thing he was actually scared of. He only tolerated them because his children had loved them, and the people needed celebrations.

* * * *

Jayne was buzzing around her newly opened shop, talking with a few customers, answering a million questions and helping teach a child how tie a shoelace. She loved this, loved sharing her little treasures, speaking with excited children and meeting other adults who were passionate about books. She'd been trying to keep as busy as she could, but her illness had hit her full force on opening day and she'd needed Dae and Mama to step in and help out. They were both worried again.

She hated that her sickness affected them so much, but there was nothing she could do about that now. Damian had made her an appointment with the medical suite at A.S.U. Now that she was officially on her way to being recognised as a member of their organisation, thanks to her work with Peter, she apparently qualified for the medical benefits that came with her new, soon-to-be official position.

She shook her head, exasperated. She'd only wanted to help, not be signed up for a new job. But she was assured that this wouldn't interfere with her day job here in her little bookstore, and that having this new title meant more advanced medical help, and access to alien doctors and healing techniques. The kind gentleman from the council who'd introduced himself as Sam had told her that although there may be nothing that could help her, he would ask his wife to see if she could at least lessen Jayne's mystery illness. She was grateful for the offer but was a little anxious about having a stranger try to heal her with special powers. She'd agreed to a medical exam, though. Damian was pleased about this, but oddly their mother wasn't.

"But you're doing so well with your current regime. Why would you change that now, and how do you know these quacks can really do anything differently, hmmm?" she'd demanded when she heard about Damian's appointment for her.

"Mama, I felt amazing for a while, but now I'm back to the same old sickly me again. If there's anyone who can help, I guess I'm willing to try. It can't hurt to talk to them, at least."

Jayne watched as she digested this then reluctantly agreed that chatting about her medical problems wouldn't hurt

Refugees

much, she supposed. Her eyes rolled when Jayne gave her a knowing smile, and she threw her hands up in the air and muttered something she couldn't quite hear then stalked off towards the coffee shop.

"I need a break. You kids want anything from the cafe?" she threw absently over her shoulder.

"Ooh, can I have a strawberry milkshake, please? Oh, and a Greek salad and some grilled chicken…"

Ashlyn turned back to her and frowned. "Well, it seems your appetite is back again. That's a good sign." She left, smiling.

Jayne did actually feel hungrier again. She'd felt so off this morning, but now she was fine. Her entire chest had been heaving with her efforts to breathe. Nothing had helped this time and it was worse, way worse than she'd ever experienced before. That was the real reason she'd agreed to see the healers. It had scared her. What if her time was nearly up?

She glanced around when Damian yelled, "You're not supposed to be here for a whole week. Are you wagging?"

"Apparently, I'm a party planner now, and His Highness decreed I get my butt back here and plan the ball next week." Peter's deep voice was gruff, but he sounded pleased too.

Jayne looked up, suddenly feeling thrilled, and smiled when she saw him.

* * * *

He stopped and stared at her. She looked…well, she looked sick. Huh. She hadn't been sick when he'd left, and it hadn't even been a full two days, yet she looked like she was dying or something.

"Ah, Damian," he turned slowly, really confused, "why is Jayne looking so sick?"

"Ah…yeah, that." Damian looked at him sheepishly then grabbed his arm. "Walk with me, would ya?" he muttered. "Okay…yeah. I didn't tell you before because, well, it wasn't your business, and then she was feeling great and normal and stuff, so I didn't think to say anything…" He was talking so fast it was hard to keep up. "But…yeah, Jayne is actually really sick. The doctors haven't ever found out why or what's causing it. Hell, they don't even have a name for whatever's happening to her. She was fine for a while there, but now it's come back again." He shrugged, not meeting Peter's eyes, and it was easy to see he was really worried.

"I didn't know." He rubbed absently at his forearm again, though it wasn't as painful as it had been earlier.

Damian frowned, watching him. "You're so weird. Did you take lessons from her or something?" He pointed to what Peter was doing.

Peter's brain stalled for a moment then he sucked in his breath raggedly. No, it wasn't possible. Jayne and Damian were biological siblings, so she couldn't be from somewhere else. Damian had told him many stories of his childhood and how his adoptive mother had found his sister and adopted her as well. This was just a coincidence, and he needed to get his head right. He needed some rest and a sumptuous meal. His mind was still hyper-alert from being in the Qualterra again. It always happened, but he didn't seem to be able to shake off his confusion.

"Huh," was all he managed before Damian was off again.

Refugees

"Yeah, so anyway, I made an appointment with the doc at headquarters, and Sam's asking his wife to come sit in on her exam. The tech here and alien healers might be able to help her or something. At this point, there's nothing to lose, right?"

It was a rhetorical question, but Peter's mind was still buzzing. Yes, that was a brilliant idea. He'd speak to Sam and his wife tonight when he saw them. He felt oddly protective of this tiny, annoying female, and now that his head was filling with nonsensical ideas, he would ask his friends for help to put it at ease.

"Cool. Hey, I actually need help with the theme for this ball. If Jayne is too unwell, could you help me?" he asked, not really expecting him to agree.

Damian did, though, surprisingly, and they walked back to A.S.U, chatting about nothing special. It seemed they were both avoiding the topic of Jayne, and probably for their own reasons.

* * * *

Damian was content having Jayne so close. He didn't like her being away from him too long. What if she needed something? At least at her store or A.S.U he could be at her side in moments if needed. Telling Peter had been hard, but he'd actually thought Jayne would already have told him. The look on his face earlier wasn't something he'd forget anytime soon; it had looked like someone had punched Peter really hard in the gut. His face was like stone and almost as grey.

It was so typical of Jayne. She'd always been the kind to suffer in silence to stop everyone else feeling bad for her. Anyone with eyes could see that Peter liked her, even though he would never admit it, so it was only fair he knew the truth, although he hadn't told Peter that she might die earlier than other people because of it, but today wasn't the right time to have that particular chat. He would have to tell Peter another day.

The appointment was set for tomorrow morning, so he would wait for any new information before deciding on what to say and when. For now, though, he would focus on anything but his sister's health worries—which was why he'd agreed to help with the ball.

"So, what kinds of balls do you all have?" he asked, not particularly interested, but if he was going to do this, he would at least do it right.

"Well, we generally theme it to a planet or species so that we can showcase each unique world's, um, culture, I guess. The foods and decorations all reflect the culture we're honouring, so we won't have a lot of time to decide. The ball's next week, on the day of remembrance. That's when we honour all who've been lost or killed before their time. We celebrate the ones who leave us from natural reasons as that's the ultimate goal, to live a long and natural life. The last one we had on our home worlds was dragon land, and it was a bit of a disaster, actually."

Peter told him how Mirren had accidentally trodden on a man and caused a small riot before the council could calm everything and everyone down again. Damian sat open-mouthed and listened raptly. If the images conjured in his mind were even slightly close to how it must've looked, he was sure no being would ever forget that ball. The problem he had now, though, was that nothing here on Earth would leave that much of an impression. He'd need a theme that was extra special if they hoped to leave a lasting impression.

Refugees

Damian's mind wandered all afternoon, trying to think of themes, but all he kept thinking was that a dragon—an actual freaking dragon—stood on some poor bugger and caused a riot. Epic. It was going to be a legend for sure. He sighed as he sat down and played with his food. Jayne was lost in thoughts of her own.

They sat in silence for a moment then both spoke at the same time.

"I don't know if—" Jayne blurted.

"Peter needs help—"

They looked at each other and laughed then Damian gestured to her to speak first.

"Okay, I wanted to say that I don't know if the appointment will help much tomorrow, because at lunch today, I started feeling better again. I know, it's really weird, but the pain just stopped, and I could breathe again. I'll still go, but I don't think we should get our hopes up for answers. I know you really want some, though," she added very gently. She flushed a little and went back to her dinner. Damian nodded thoughtfully, but didn't comment on that.

"Okay, my turn. I need your help. Peter has to come up with an earthly theme for this ball, and we don't have a lot of time. So, Miss Smarty Pants, wanna help me come up with a theme that none of these aliens will forget anytime soon?" He threw her a grin; he was hoping to rock this ball.

"Well," she started, "what other themes have they done?"

Damian went into the details Peter had shared that afternoon, and Jayne was held just as rapt by the stories as he'd been. He also explained the significance of these celebrations.

She nodded solemnly, chewing her food absently, then swallowed before answering. "Well, that's easy. We should make it a masquerade ball." She rolled her eyes at him. Clearly, he should've known that was the obvious choice here.

"Aww, really? I thought that might be a bit boring and, well…safe, you know?" He gestured with his arms to show that the other balls had been better by far.

"You're such a goose, Dae. The whole reason to go understated and safe is to stand out. Every other ball has had some catastrophic event. We want to have a safe ball, with nothing dangerous happening. It will show that we can party and be elegant and be safe and secure all at the same time." She sat back to look at him.

She was right. That would make them stand out. "Kitty, you're the best. While you're seeing the doctors tomorrow, I'll put together some pics for Peter. You should've told him you're ill, though. He was pretty crushed today when he found out."

* * * *

He what? She opened her mouth, but he cut her off.

"He has a right to know. Everyone can see he likes you. Stop being so stubborn and just tell him." He threw her a sharp look, something he rarely did.

She nodded, not really wanting him to know she was scared of how Peter would react, and they finished eating in silence.

Chapter 35

Jayne tossed and turned all night, dreaming about giant feet and weird balls held outdoors in places she didn't know but somehow recognised. It was just from all the stories Dae had told her, with her mind making up a few of its own. There was a silver-haired king in several who seemed to know her, and of course the people she'd met so far at A.S.U were there as well. In one part of her dream, the woman Angel had been standing off in a corner with an oddly dark expression on her face. The memory made Jayne shiver as she got up to shower. Since meeting her a short time ago, Jayne always felt cold when she thought of Angel, though there was no actual reason for it.

Jayne sighed softly as she undressed and turned on the water. Her brother would be up and ready by now. There really wasn't any point delaying the inevitable, but she hated doctors. Well, actually, it was having to go through her entire medical history only to be told there was no reason for her to be this sickly that she hated. Or even worse, they could put it down to her accident.

She let the hot water run over her hair and thought about Peter—it was easier than thinking of her dreams and how Angel gave her the willies every time she came near her. Or thought about her. He was going to be mad that she hadn't told him about her illness, but it wasn't his business anyway.

Today she would wear a red curly wig and deep blue power suit. Nothing said "I'm fine" quite like that, and she didn't want anyone to think differently. Choosing her eye colour would be a little harder. She finally settled for a set of grey contacts, plain and soft, which wouldn't distract from her suit. She carefully got ready, trying to avoid sudden movements in case it triggered another episode.

As she dressed, she hummed a little melody she'd always known but couldn't quite place. None of her searches had found the song either, which probably meant she was remembering the words all wrong. She put light makeup on, keeping her look neutral and soft, with just a hint of eyeliner, and was pleased with the outcome. The red curls bounced softly and came to her waist, and she clipped a small piece at the front with a glittery butterfly then pinned a quirky brooch her mother had gotten for her to the lapel of her suit. She left her neck bare and added her favourite perfume, which smelled like vanilla sweets. She chose a simple ballet flat, dark blue with tiny flowers sewn onto them then grabbed a small clutch and went down for breakfast.

* * * *

Damian was already eating breakfast when Jayne came downstairs. He appraised her and raised an eyebrow. "Well, aren't you the Scottish boss then?"

She laughed at him. "I didn't want to be so loud today. I figured being more sophisticated would reassure you that I'm taking this appointment today very seriously." She tried for a serious voice but didn't quite make it.

He frowned at her. "Kitty, for once, can you be worried about you, please? It's hard when we're all terrified and you are totally blasé." He took a sip of coffee and sighed when she looked at him sourly. "Okay, well can you at least pretend to be worried for my sake then? Please?"

Refugees

      Jayne ate quietly after that, seemingly lost in her own thoughts.

      He took their empty dishes to the kitchen and rinsed them.

* * * *

      Jayne was waiting by the car for him when he finally emerged, and she slid in quietly, not wanting to argue but also not feeling very calm. She twisted her hands and gave Dae a soft smile as he got in and looked over at her.

      He nodded. "Okay, let's do this."

      The drive to A.S.U wasn't a very long one, but the traffic today was heavier than usual, so it took them about twenty minutes longer to get there. Thankfully, they'd left very early so they made it just in time for her appointment.

      As Damian filled out her paperwork, a nurse came and collected her to check her weight, height, and vitals. She explained to Jayne that they would be doing some blood tests and scans as well, so if she had any piercings and jewellery on she would need to remove them. She gave Jayne a plastic clip bag to keep her stuff in when it was time. She came back to the waiting room as Damian finished her paperwork at the desk. He made his way over to her. She'd chosen a little couch right at the back that didn't look as dreadful as the hard, plastic chairs, though it was just as uncomfortable.

      Damian sat next to her and started scrolling through his phone, checking his messages and texting. She was way too nervous to do the same, so she sat there like a statue and twisted her fingers until they hurt. Just as she'd decided to get some water, the doctor called her in. Well, at least her wait wasn't that long. Damian got up automatically and followed her, slipping his phone into his top pocket as they went.

The doctor was a lovely man. He shook her hand carefully and Damian's heartily then introduced himself as Isaac. The healer's name was Evaliah, but she preferred Eva. She was the beautiful long-haired woman Jayne had seen that first day in the meeting room, the one who'd rushed to the equally beautiful blonde Damian seemed to like so much, Hannah.

"Hello," was all she could utter, she was so nervous.

"Okay, Jayne, we're gonna get right into it, if that's okay with you? I've had a thorough look at your records, but there was a lot to go through, so if I miss something, you just tell me." He patted her hand then turned to the files on his desk and opened them.

They talked for over an hour, going through her history, and every now and again, from the corner of her eye, she saw Eva look at her oddly. Maybe that was just her normal way of examining someone though. Then Isaac did a physical examination and sent her for blood tests and some X-rays to check her chest. According to him, all her previous ones were distorted and almost impossible to read. She nodded. This wasn't news to her. They'd tried everything, but for some reason the machines just went fuzzy.

After a few hours of poking and prodding, she was put onto a new medication to help with her breathing. It had only been released a short time ago and wasn't on the market for the general population yet. He was hopeful it would at least ease her chest tightness. Then it was the healer's turn to examine her. This was the bit she'd been worrying about the most. She didn't know what to expect and that made her more anxious than seeing the new doctor.

Refugees

Eva gently placed a hand on her forehead and asked her to close her eyes and relax. She did, and felt a tiny jolt, but it didn't hurt at all. Then the older woman repeated this on her back, arms, legs, and tummy. The brief jolts reminded her of a massage, the kind where the electrical wand passed over you gave you little zaps to invigorate the body.

"Hmm, you're responding very well," she said at last, and Jayne looked at her in confusion. "It's all right, dear. That's a really good thing. It's just odd that a human being would get so much comfort from my abilities. It's been a challenge to heal humans so far. We can't heal them as well as we can beings who have magix." She eyed Jayne curiously for a moment then smiled at her. "Well, I've done what I can for now. You've had a lot of trauma to your body and organs, so I think you'll benefit from several sessions to help you get the most from the healing. It's good you seem to respond so well to my ability. Are you sure you're from here originally, dear?" she added softly.

Damian blinked rapidly then laughed. "We're biological siblings, so…yeah. I was adopted by our mom a few years before we found my sister. Our mom was close friends with our biological mother before she died." Eva said nothing but nodded thoughtfully. He turned to his sister. "Are you ready? We can grab some lunch then go tell Mom how your day was."

She nodded. "Yes, that sounds really good." And it did. Her stomach was growling. She turned to both the healer and the doctor. "Thank you. I came here expecting nothing to change, but I do feel a bit better now. I'll stop and get my new medicine before I go as well." She shook hands with both of them.

Dae held the door open for her.

They strolled to the café and got their lunches to go, as well as a brownie and coffee for Ashlyn. It was late in the afternoon now, and their mother was working the shop so Jayne could see the doctors. Ashlyn looked up as they came in, her phone up to her ear, and quickly said her goodbyes before clipping it shut and coming to hug her children.

"So, how'd it go today?" She checked Jayne over like she was looking for scratches or something but spoke to Damian.

"Really well, actually, Mama," Jayne said loudly. She wanted her mother to ask her about her appointment, not her brother.

Ashlyn smiled and kissed her forehead lightly. "That's excellent news, honey. I'm happy it went well. Did they find a name or reason for your illness yet? Or maybe they're thinking of naming it something completely new." She was teasing a bit and Jayne giggled.

"No, they don't know what it is, but the healer really helped. She even asked if I was an alien cause she could do so much for me, but Dae set her straight."

* * * *

Ashlyn must've lost control of her expression for an instant, because when she looked at Damian, he was staring at her, frowning. She took a breath and opened her mouth, but Damian shook his head. She nodded. They would discuss it later. Jayne kept up a constant babble of chatter for the rest of the afternoon, and when they left, Ashlyn followed them home. She would have to tell at least Damian now, and it was better to do it where Jayne was more settled and distracted. She looked exhausted after today.

Refugees

As Damian got changed, Ashlyn washed up the few dishes in the sink then tidied the kitchen and wiped down the counters. Jayne was yawning now, and Ashlyn suggested she go get into bed. She would make some cocoa and bring it up, but she suspected Jayne would be fast asleep before it was ready. Jayne rubbed her eyes and yawned again, hugged her mother, and went up to her room.

* * * *

Damian looked at his mother for a minute, his hair standing on end. He'd always had a sense there was stuff she hadn't told them, but now he would get answers from her.

She turned and looked at him, threw her hands up, and gathered herself. "We're aliens. Our people were slaughtered, all of them. They came in the middle of the night, so many of them, and slaughtered every man, woman, and child they could find. Some of us had been off looking for the Great Ones and were on other worlds when it happened. We felt it. What happened was so brutal we felt a psychic link to our people across the universe…" Her voice broke, but she drew in a deep breath and continued. "So…my husband wasn't with me when it happened. He was at home. I snuck in after the initial attack and started searching for him, and I found Amanda, your mother. We were close growing up, but we'd drifted apart by the time she married and had kids, though we still wrote letters.

"Anyway, she was barely alive…but she recognised me and begged me to keep you safe from the Huntowra. She said they'd already killed your sister and couldn't bear to think of them getting you too, so I took you and ran. We knew we could come here, and had papers crafted for your adoption when we got here, the place that arranged adoptions creates DNA profiles to keep track of the children. That's how we found out that

Jayne is your actual sister." She stopped to stifle another sob. "As far as we knew, she'd died." She fidgeted with the tea towel and kept her gaze on the floor. "There's something off about her magix, though. It's been seeping away from her, and I think that's why she's sick. She needs to go back home and have her power read by the magix ring. She was too young to have had her full magix when we found her, and the ring is the only safe place to release power like that…"

"You should have told me," he spat. "I work with them every day, and you never told me I'm one of them. Or that my sister's illness is linked somehow to magix. She could've died!"

Damian's head was spinning. He was so hurt and confused. Why not tell them the truth? And why did he feel fine, but she didn't? There were so many questions he didn't know where to start. And then his mind caught up. The Huntowra had wiped them out in the middle of the night? So then he was… He sucked in a sudden breath, and Ashlyn looked up.

"Are we… Are we Aggaron?"

"Yes. And if anyone finds out we aren't all dead, everyone here will die with us. The Huntowra exterminated our race because we're a major threat to them, Damian. We've been training and preparing to attack them, but to do that, we first need to gather as many as we can, to gather our strength and then hit them head on at the last minute."

Damian's mouth hung open. "How many? How many of our people are alive and hiding and training to fight back?" It was meant to be a rhetorical question, but she answered him.

"Nearly five thousand. We were scattered and went into hiding as soon as we felt it. A few get caught from time to time, but everyone now thinks we're an extinct race." She crossed her

Refugees

arms defensively and looked him right in the eye. "Damian, someone's working against us. Helping the Huntowra. That's the only way they could've known our people's locations and when we would be most vulnerable. Please, please don't tell anyone we're here and alive. If they know, word will get back to the Huntowra, and none of us will stand a chance. I need you to keep this secret with me. You can be angry and ask me anything, but please, help me protect what's left of our people."

Damian nodded unconsciously, and she sighed with relief. "Okay. But, Mom, we have to tell A.S.U something. They already suspect she's...we are alien. Would it matter if we said we just don't know where we're from? We could sell that. They knew from the start about our amnesia, and this would let them help her but keep us hidden." He was pacing, thinking of ways to tell them without giving out too much information.

Ashlyn shook her head. "No, Damian. If we said you were both alien, they'd want to know how I knew that. They'd want to question me and then they'd know who I am. I can't hide my identity. Troy was a very well-known, high-ranking warrior and a senior member of the council. It's a fluke nobody's recognised me, but if we tell them that we're alien, they might put those pieces together." She was twisting her hands together as Jayne had done earlier today. "What if you don't tell them, but let them figure it out themselves? Then you can plausibly deny knowledge and they're none the wiser about me and the rest? Do you think that could work?"

"Well, Evaliah already outright asked—"

"Crap. Evaliah? Oh crap... She's only the best healer in the entire universe." Ashlyn gestured around her frantically, her voice so high pitched it was nearly inaudible, then calmed and chewed her nails as she thought. "Okay. No, that's good. Go to her and ask her why she thought Jayne was an alien. It will get her thinking about it. Then drop hints here and there, tell her you don't know your past, so you could be an alien. That type of thing. Then let them figure it out."

"Mom, you know I don't like lying. I think I should just say nothing and let them ask me. I'll answer as best I can and be vague. Okay?"

Ashlyn nodded then glanced at her watch. It was getting late, so she said her goodbyes.

Refugees

Chapter 36

Peter was standing alone in the meeting room when Eva found him. She looked tired.

"There you are. I've been searching everywhere." She gave him a soft kiss on the cheek as she had when he was a child, though now she had to reach up to do it.

He grimaced. Exhaustion seeped off her like a curtain blowing in the breeze. The Starling Trumpets gently shifted and twinkled behind her as she faced him.

"Peter, you're right about the girl. She's not human, but neither she nor her brother have any awareness of their true selves, and I'm worried about it. It would take a significant trauma, or repeated traumas, to cause that damage to the girl. I couldn't even heal her in one sitting. It will take me several attempts, and even then, I may not be able to undo all of it. Also, when I was healing her, something else happened." Her brow furrowed, and she stared off into the distance, seeming to forget for a moment that he was there. "Peter, I saw something… I think it was a memory of hers."

"What? How is that possible? What was it?"

"Well, it was a face. A hideous Huntowra face, laughing at her, and then she fell—he let her go, actually—and then pain exploded everywhere, and the memory was gone. I can't understand it. I even felt her agony… I've never experienced the feelings and memories of another. I think that perhaps whatever drained all her magix has done this too." She shrugged. She was trying to hide it, but he could tell she was worried and confused.

"Wait, what do you mean she's been drained of her magix? How has that happened? She's not human, but she's been here her whole life. And her brother has as well." He dragged a hand through his messy hair in frustration. "So, that means there are rips to this world. We need to know where from. I'll talk with Damian when I see him next. He deserves to know that he's not human, that they—" He snapped his mouth shut then when the door opened. He didn't want this conversation to get out, and Evaliah seemed to understand because she looked at him and nodded, interpreting his silence correctly.

Angel and two soldiers walked in, stopping when they saw Peter and Evaliah standing near the ring. "Oh, are you coming with us, Peter?" Angel asked. Her voice was soft as a whisper, but there was a chill about it.

"I'm sorry, but no. I was lost in my own thoughts when Evaliah here found me and asked if I was okay. My friend's been unwell, and I was worried for her. Evaliah tried to heal her…well, as best as she could anyway." He offered her a smile that wasn't quite genuine, but she didn't seem to notice.

Her perfect features blurred slightly for a moment before she answered, "Oh. Is that the strange human girl you're so fond—"

The ring hummed, and a portal opened in the squared area. Everyone was still in the square as the energy fields came up all around them. Then, before any of them had time to ask what was happening, there was an explosive sound and his team appeared right in front of them, holding onto chains with an angry Huntowra trying to escape them. Someone closed the

Refugees

portal, and they subdued the creature.

Peter looked at all the faces. "What in the stars happened here?"

Angel snorted indignantly, and Evaliah just stood there staring.

"Well, we got into a fight after you left. These bastards snuck up on us and tried to ambush us, but thanks to your great hearing, we were prepared. Well, most of us were anyway," Travis said dryly and pointed to Bryant's face.

He was covered in blood and his nose looked broken, but other than that, he seemed okay. Evaliah reached out to him and touched his face, absorbing the damage and healing him in a moment.

"Thanks, Eva," Bryant muttered and flashed her a boyish grin before turning his attention back to his brother. "I got the son of a bitch. He slipped up, and I was right behind him. Punched him out cold." He puffed out his chest. "He got me in the face with his wing, though."

The room didn't quieten down for a while. Everyone was telling their versions of the battle, and the Huntowra stared at each of them in disgust. Angel moved back, and Peter stepped in front of her automatically to block her from view.

"Get it out of here," he demanded as the energy fields faded away.

Caleb and Bryant hauled the Huntowra off to the holding cells on the upper floor. The creature shrank back at the Starling Trumpets, hissing furiously and trying to free itself, but with all the chains and clamps on its wings, there was no escape.

Peter looked at Angel. He was about to ask her if she

was okay, but the look on her face caught him off guard. He could only describe it as murderous. She was staring after the Huntowra, seemingly unaware of being watched.

She blinked and her face cleared, her smile back in place again. "I think that, given this, I should travel another day, Peter."

He frowned but nodded, lost for words, and watched as she walked away. He turned to see if anyone else needed his help, but they were all busy talking amongst themselves.

Travis rubbed his jaw and muttered to nobody in particular, "Well, I'm gonna go check on Seth. He'll wanna know everything, and he'll be excited when he sees the faces of the Five that Caleb drew. This bastard is one of them, you know." He pointed in the direction of the cell. "We'd just looked at the pictures when he attacked. I thought it was a fluke at first, but I'm not so sure now." He strode out to find Seth, still muttering to himself.

* * * *

Seth and Jye were playing poker. Jye took his poker face seriously, which made Seth laugh, which made him wince again.

"You shouldn't laugh if it hurts that much, Seth. Your body needs rest. I don't even know why I let you talk me into playing cards when you should be sleeping." He sighed a little and moved as though he were about to get up.

Seth reached out, panicked, and blurted, "Sorry. I won't do it again, just stay here, okay?"

Was this fear from being attacked and tortured, or was he worried about Travis? Or possibly a bit of both? Jye nodded

Refugees

calmly and settled back in his position at the end of Seth's bed. Just then the doors swung open and Travis came in, followed by Bryant, who was bloodied and a little bruised, although he'd clearly been healed. It looked like someone had punched him in the face. Jye wasn't surprised; he had a tendency to rub people the wrong way. The two men didn't speak to each other as they walked toward the back of the hospital room, weaving past empty beds and coming to a stop in front of Seth.

"So, we came home early, clearly, and we even brought home a surprise," Travis said dryly. His face screwed up like he'd sucked on a lemon, and his gaze darted to Jye and then away before he could read anything in them. "While we were away, we got Caleb to do some sketches for us. Emma described the Elite Five Huntowra from her childhood, and he spent hours drawing them. They're not perfect, I imagine, but they're close representations of who we need to be extra careful of. And we caught one—"

"Hey, man, that was me. I caught him. I'm awesome," Bryant butted in.

Travis rolled his eyes then continued as though there'd been no interruption. "So we wanted to show you these bad-ass drawings, and I was thinking we should add the one who tortured you to the list of extra-crazy Huntowra to be careful around." He shrugged.

"Sure, I guess." Seth looked at Jye anxiously, and Jye nodded in encouragement. This might be good for him. Give him a chance to work through his ordeal, and his fear. "So how does this work then?"

"Well, first I'll show you the drawings so you can see the kinds of details we're looking for, and then Caleb can sit with you and you can describe your attacker. We can do it now or whenever you're ready. Do you feel up to it?"

"I'm okay, Trav. A bit shaken, yeah, but I'll be okay. Now, let's see these monster mugshots." He drew in a shaky breath.

Travis reached into his backpack, brought out rolled-up pieces of paper, one at a time, and set them on the bed between Seth and Jye. Then he drew up a chair and sat right in the middle.

"So, anyone okay to start with or is there an order?" Seth asked sarcastically, his usual response to fear.

Travis smiled and nodded.

Seth reached out and grabbed a random scroll. "Argh, that dude's so gross." He cringed as he stared at the picture of the Huntowra. He threw the scroll down and reached for another one.

Jye picked up the first to look at it. The Huntowra's entire left side was disfigured and heavily scarred on his face and neck, and his wing was bent at a funny angle, like it had been damaged and never set properly. He stared at the face and shuddered.

"Yeah, bro, we got that bastard and locked him up. He ain't hurting nobody no more." Bryant clapped Jye on the shoulder and practically drove him into the ground with the force of his shove. "Oops, sorry," he said sheepishly.

Jye didn't respond. How terrifying the whole kidnapping must've been for Emma. He'd never considered how brutal they were before now, and it mortified him. She'd been so brave, trying to fight them off, and this was only one of them. He looked up as Seth opened the next scroll, gagged, and

Refugees

threw it down where the first one had been. This one had long hair and wore it tied back, off his face. He was very strong looking, but his eyes were hideous. Jye didn't even pick the paper up to look.

The next one looked very similar, and they all wondered aloud if it was possible for the Huntowra to have twins. They hadn't heard of any before. Next was a doe-eyed, wiry looking Huntowra that looked almost sickly, but there was a deep hatred in his eyes that terrified them all. They spent a while talking about how it made them feel, and Seth was smiling wryly when he unrolled the last scroll.

His expression froze and all the blood drained from his face. He gulped, and waves of his terror flooded Jye. He dropped into a protective crouch, his desire to shove everyone away from Seth almost impossible to fight. His stripes started flashing.

"Seth?" Jye choked out, his strangled voice breaking. "What's wrong brother?"

"It's him," Seth murmured, his eyes filling. "That's him, the one who…"

The entire room felt like it had chilled in less than a minute. Jye held out his hand for the picture with tears in his own eyes. The pain he felt was his own and Seth's, and it was crushing him. "It's okay. You're safe here with us," he murmured reassuringly to Seth.

He took the paper from him and stared at the face. He was easily the most dangerous-looking of the group. His eyebrows were angled oddly, and his eyes and hair were an inky black. He was muscular and reasonably tall, and he wore a necklace with what looked like fingers, claws, and teeth on it.

196

His chest was left bare other than this. His mouth was set in a permanent snarl, and he wore the expression of a fanatic. Whatever he was doing, it was something he believed in passionately, and that made him more dangerous than the others.

Bile rose in Jye's throat and he threw the picture onto the bed. Both Bryant and Travis stared in horror at it, not daring to pick it up. It took a minute for the nausea to pass and Jye to stop feeling dizzy. Anger like nothing he'd ever felt before overwhelmed him, but he dared not move in case he hurt Seth.

After a few minutes of silence, Bryant huffed, "Well, I gotta go sit in on the questioning, but first I need to get changed." Without saying goodbye, he turned and strode out of the hospital wing.

"Yeah. Actually, I should go and let the boss know about these." Travis pointed to the pictures "He'll wanna see them too, I guess. They are guilty of killing his kid, after all." Keeping his eyes down, he scooped up the scrolls before shooting a last quick look at Jye.

* * * *

When they were alone again, Seth levelled a glare at Jye, who blinked in surprise.

"What?" he demanded. "What did I do?"

"Don't you realise?" He took a breath. "Trav likes you, Jye. Go ask him out for a coffee or something."

Jye laughed, glad for the change of subject. "Oh, yeah, that. I mean, I guessed. I was thinking I'd ask him to come to the ball, you know, if he likes that sort of thing…but we haven't even been told the theme for this year yet."

Refugees

Peter appeared out of nowhere and strode to the bed. It had happened a lot the last couple of days. The brothers all came to check on their newest family member, even though, technically, he was only Jye's new family member. It was kind of nice having people care about him. A family. He'd never had that before, really, apart from Travis and his dad.

"Actually, that's why I'm here. The theme is masquerade."

Seth goggled at him. How had he known what they were talking about?

"I can hear you from everywhere," he teased his brother and winked at Seth. "If you need to, you can google it, but it's formal and everyone wears a mask to hide their identity. It could be kind of fun, actually. Mirren's sulking and might come looking for someone to sympathise with him. He's been told human form only for the ball." Peter and Jye winced at the same time, and Seth watched them curiously. He'd ask Jye about it later.

"After the last one, he's lucky he's invited at all," Jye answered in a menacing tone, clearly still upset by whatever had happened, which only increased Seth's curiosity.

Chapter 37

Emma, Caleb, and Bryant were in a room with a one-way mirror, waiting for the interrogation of the Huntowra to begin. Nausea filled Emma, and it was all she could do not to gag. She hadn't really expected to come face-to-face with any of the Elite Five again, despite her desire to get revenge for Lilah. She grimaced, remembering the face of the one she'd injured. This wasn't him, though.

Caleb was sitting back with his feet up on the wall, munching on a pack of chips, and Bryant was standing in the centre of the glass, looking straight at the Huntowra, his body stiff and alert like he expected it to leap through the glass at any minute. It couldn't, of course. There were barriers surrounding the room and then more the hall, and still more protecting the entire building. With all those and an ever-growing number of Starling Trumpets around the place, this Huntowra wasn't going anywhere in a hurry.

Some military men and elders arrived to conduct the interrogation. The elders needed to be present so they could translate for the humans, and to defuse any attempt to escape.

"Alrighty then, let's get started, shall we?" said the heavyset, middle-aged military man, who sat directly in front of the Huntowra, his moustache moving up and down with every word.

The Huntowra glared at him then looked over at Tobias, the elder who leaned against the far wall facing to the door.

Refugees

Tobias looked sternly at the Huntowra then spoke, the magix translating in an instant. "It is beginning. We are here to question you about the attack you attempted in the Qualterra," he said smoothly, but there was a steely edge to his words and a sharp glint in his eyes.

"You are not worthy of knowing anything. You're pathetic and weak, and you only captured me by accident. There was no actual skill involved," he snarled.

Bryant snorted. "The hell it was luck. I had to sneak around two other Huntowra to get in the right spot to wait for this one." He jabbed his finger at the window, staring ahead the whole time.

It soon became obvious that this Huntowra had a lot of pride and was easily offended when he wasn't given credit. This gave the interrogators an idea. Moustache, who's name was Mark, started to throw out insults, with Tobias translating so the Huntowra knew it. It didn't take long before he was spitting out cuss words and demanding they all surrender.

"I am Kyden of the Elite Five. I do not cower or fear scum like you," he spat with disgust. "You will all fall when the betrayer among you finds out you hold me here. The betrayer answers only to her, the most feared queen of all." He glared at them all in turn.

"Who does this betrayer answer to?" Tobias asked before anyone had the chance to. His voice was deadly quiet now, but he stood up straight, his eyes narrowed.

"The betrayer answers to the one who rules the twelve and makes them cower like spineless beasts." He snapped his jaw shut then, his teeth clacking audibly. He seemed to realise he'd said something he shouldn't have and crossed his arms, a gesture of defiance. He refused to speak again, and after another half an hour, they returned him to his holding cell, and Tobias filled them in on what the Huntowra had said.

"Well, that was surprising," Moustache said absently. "Either he's lying and trying to set us up, or he just let some precious intel slip." He twirled the ends of his moustache around his finger, apparently digesting the information.

* * * *

Tobias stared intently at the now-empty chair.

"We should have a chat with the emperor and let him know, but we shouldn't tell anyone else about this. These kinds of things always cause more problems. We'll need to find this…betrayer as quickly as possible."

"How? How do we find someone who can clearly mask their true intentions and walk among us so freely?"

"That's the easy part, sonny." Mark grimaced. "We'll have two or three lots of intel and slip it to different groups. That will narrow it down to a few, and then we separate them further once we know who to feed false intel to."

Tobias blinked. "I don't think that will do any good though, Mark. They'll know from the start it's false intel."

"Sonny, we're gonna set up an elaborate ruse. First, we mark locations where we know there's no Huntowra presence, and make an excuse why we need teams to head out to those spots. They'll stay there for three days, which is a short scouting mission but plausible. Then we mark which team is A, B, and C. Then we tell team A where team C is headed. Team B we give the location of team A, and C we say where team B is. Then we repeat with different teams until we get a hit. That will

Refugees

narrow the list from over a hundred potential spies down to just five—or seven, depending on the scout sizes." Mark shrugged. He'd obviously used this tactic before at some point.

Tobias still wasn't sure it would work but let it drop. He had more important things to attend to right now. "Okay, I'll fill the others in. We have a meeting anyway to discuss the ever-growing number of refugees coming in." He sighed, rubbing his stubbled chin and yawned as he straightened up to leave, his back popping.

Tobias knocked quietly on the door and entered the meeting. He was late because of the interrogation, but they'd expected he would be. He looked at the faces around the room and smiled grimly then took his seat. Someone was talking about repairs to the castle on Meakra, which had been made a priority because the castle grounds and buildings were large enough to house several hundred people and could be used as a base.

"And what about the girl's idea? If we can stop the Huntowra from using their wings, we would be far better off, and repairs would be safer and use fewer people since we wouldn't need such a large guard."

Tobias rolled his eyes. The woman's idea had caused lots of debate, and it frustrated him that everything came down to doing what was easier or with fewer people. In his opinion, their safety was always the most important thing.

"Tobias, you don't agree?" Matthew looked at Tobias with curiosity.

Tobias cleared his throat. "With all due respect, Majesty, I don't. If we want to ensure that the people working to repair our homes are safe, we shouldn't rely on tricks or gimmicks in place of manpower. It should be our responsibility and priority to be with them as they work. I think it's worth the effort for peace of mind and in case anything goes wrong. I don't mean that we should dismiss the idea—stopping them from using their wings would be terrific—but we need to add that to our existing strategy, to beef up our defences, as the humans would say." He chewed his nail absently and looked only at the emperor. It didn't matter that the others had differing opinions; he was used to being unpopular.

Matthew considered him for a minute then made a soft sound in his throat. "What did I say, Tobias? Call me Matt here. I am your emperor, that's true, but I'm also a warrior and a refugee, just as you are. Just as everyone here is." He gestured around at the room. "I agree with you, actually. It's important that we show our people we're all in this together and working as hard as they are to restore our homes and lives."

The entire room was quiet, and everyone was watching Matthew. This was why he was the most popular of the royals. He was passionate and blunt, and not at all interested in formality during a crisis. The rest of the meeting went smoothly, and when he informed them of the spy amongst them, it didn't really surprise anyone. Unlikely things had happened often enough that they'd suspected something was amiss, such as Huntowra showing up in a place they shouldn't have been, apparently by chance. This was an enormous threat, though, and they took it seriously, laying out plans to catch whoever was working to betray them.

Chapter 38

"Okay, guys, listen up. There are some missions coming up, and we aren't allowed to say why, only that they need us to act as security on possible Huntowra bases in three-day shifts. This will happen for a while before we decide if the intel is accurate or if we should redirect our energies elsewhere. We will be rotated randomly and not given new intel until the mission starts, in case a team gets caught. All team leaders are in the same situation, so we know nothing more than you do." Travis stared hard at each face, having a hard time believing that any of them would betray them all. He'd worked with most of them, trained a few, and was even friends with several of them.

Bryant was hanging around the edges of the room. He'd already briefed his group, including Seth and Jye. He was normally loud and obnoxious, but not today. He'd been very serious since the interrogation of the Huntowra. It was almost frightening to see the difference in his demeanour, but also rather inspiring. This was a man Travis felt safe working with, and he felt a stab of remorse for not really liking Bryant much before now, for not allowing himself to see that this man had a whole other side to him. He had always seemed too relaxed, and even a little too loud, to be an effective warrior, but clearly the persona he showed was the one he wanted people to see, not the real him.

Travis gave him a slight smile and nodded as he picked up the chairs that had recently been vacated.

"Want a hand there, bud?" Bryant seemed less than enthusiastic, but he nodded and kept going.

Bryant fell in beside him and quietly cleared away the rest of the chairs, not even bothering to speak. It was as though he needed the quiet as much as Travis did. After the chairs were all packed away, Travis sighed.

"Wanna help me vacuum?" It was a half-hearted joke, but Bryant shrugged, nodded.

Travis looked at him for a minute. Something was up. "Bryant, what's going on?" he said softly.

"I reckon I have an idea about who," he looked around and lowered his voice even more, "about who's been working for the other side." He fidgeted and swallowed hard then rubbed his neck in frustration. His short hair was sticking out at weird angles like he hadn't brushed it in days. "It's just a few minor things, really, and I don't wanna involve anyone else, cause I'm sure I'm right. I don't wanna give anyone a chance to run. But they can read thoughts so I need help from someone who isn't as closely monitored, you know…just in case." He eyed Travis with embarrassment, and he understood. Bryant was asking for help to set a separate trap for the betrayer with no one else the wiser.

"What are we gonna do?" He squared his shoulders and looked right at Bryant and saw the relief on his face.

"Well, we need to feed some random false intel of our own, but in a way that only someone in particular will hear. So it has to be that we have a pre-mission meet and let this intel slip, with us apparently none the wiser. Then they'll take that and send it to the Huntowra. As soon as we do this, they'll know we're on to them. It's a one-shot deal. I already have Peter working on something for it. He's the only other one who knows, and he agrees about this person." Bryant straightened up, which was apparently his way of ending the discussion.

"Okay, let me know when and what." He turned back to the vacuum, knowing Bryant would leave now. He had some of his bounce back after saying what was bothering him.

Travis put all thought from his head and focused on his pointless task. It helped numb all the tumultuous emotions swirling inside him. After a short while, he hummed, and his mind drifted to Jye. He'd asked him to come round for dinner and was mentally planning what to make. His cooking wasn't the best, but he knew a few things that were fool proof and tasty too.

"Travis." A soft voice made him jump, and he turned, confused.

"Mmm?" He looked at his visitor. Angel. "Oh, hey, Angel. What's up?" He didn't speak to her often, so it surprised him that she knew his name at all.

"Oh, umm, I was wondering something. I wanted to go to a, well, a pub, I think it's called. The ones that do dinners. But I don't know which one is the best to visit. I thought since you're human, you might know of a good one."

Travis was taken aback. This seemed like such an odd question, especially since Angel didn't like....well, anything. And then it clicked. She was the one betraying them. The instant he thought it, she hissed at him. Her beautiful, calm face seemed to crackle and become ugly for a second and then she turned and fled.

"Bryant! Bryant, she's taken off!" Somehow, he knew that Bryant was close, and that he'd hear.

He barely got the words out when a streak of colour jumped down the stairs two at a time and took off up the hall after her.

"It's okay. We knew this would happen." Peter appeared at his shoulder.

Travis grabbed at his chest, rubbing it in circles to slow his heart rate. "Shit, what the hell, man? You're gonna give me a heart attack at this rate."

The sun had nearly set, and the lamps lit themselves. Then suddenly Peter was drawing random lines on the magix square, muttering to himself while he did it. Travis wanted to ask what was happening, but he didn't want to break his concentration.

He'd been the bait, the 'oops' moment in this little ruse. He laughed involuntarily, impressed by the whole setup.

Peter looked up at him and tilted his head. "Are you okay, Travis?" he asked, seeming genuinely concerned. "Uh, yeah. Just didn't expect to be the bait, that's all. It's fine, though. Hopefully I didn't screw it up much."

"You did perfectly. We had no time to prepare you beforehand. Unfortunately, she was already onto us. I knew you would put the pieces together quickly and that would be an advantage, but I'm sorry we did that to you without asking."

Travis smiled grimly. "It's fine. Sorry I let her escape, though. I sure hope that Bryant can catch her."

Peter actually laughed. "Don't worry. My brother might be a goof, but he's also an incredible tracker. So good, in fact, that the trackers want him to train the newbies full time, but Bryant's sense of doing right is so strong that sitting aside and training others feels like he's not living up to his full potential." Peter's lips thinned. "Ironic that he's one of the best trackers who ever existed, yet he's not interested in the job."

It dawned on Travis that there was much more to Bryant than he'd ever known. If he was the best, why hadn't he been there to find Seth? Surely they would have wanted him? Had he been busy with another mission? His mind swam with possibilities, and he felt dizzy.

* * * *

Bryant had narrowed down the number of places where Angel could be hiding. It had been a few hours now. She was damn good at evasion. He smirked, and a low snarl slipped through his teeth, which were clenched with excitement. Bryant hadn't had a challenge in a very long time. This was giving him a strange sense of satisfaction.

He also worried. She'd been cornered and busted now, so there was no reason for her not to lash out at the innocent people around her. He didn't know how far she would go. Was she capable of actually killing a human? She was so small, physically, but clearly she wasn't normal. He would need to be careful. See for himself how strong she was. It would be foolish to underestimate her.

He jumped from the rooftops stealthily, watching the humans bustling below with no idea of the danger they were in. He sometimes wished he could be so clueless. It must be nice not to worry about extermination. The streets were still busy. Shoppers walked in every direction with their purchases, and sidewalk cafes sparkled with candles and soft, romantic lights. He loved the cafés. Maybe one day he could bring someone special here, just to experience them.

He scanned for Angel. She was near, of that he was sure. He moved to the next set of rooftops and started scanning again, still finding nothing.

This would be a long night. The only plus was that he could still sense her presence.

Chapter 39

Her rage was more profound than anything she'd felt in a very long time. In all her years, she'd never lost it like this, the rage taking her over so she was nothing more than a spectator in her own body. The glamour she used to conceal her true self was still intact, so she decided on a whim to find something to hunt. Perhaps a brutal message for these pathetic meat-sacks would give her time to escape. She needed to warn Nosk of what was happening, and soon. They were running out of time, and they had everything to lose by waiting longer.

She started running in circles, looking for her target. She came across an out-of-the-way bar on the edge of this godforsaken city and watched, fascinated by the hapless people falling about, bodies filled with poisonous liquids and smoke. Some were mating against a wall while another was puking in a nearby rubbish bin. She was about to leave when one stumbled out into the street. He was short and kind of waddled, one of his feet turning in slightly. His eyes were set far apart, odd even by human standards, and his short, greasy hair had flakes of scalp in it, a common affliction for humans. This one was particularly slow but didn't seem overly poisoned. He was counting sizeable amounts of money, not paying attention to where he was, and had to start over a couple of times. He stopped in a deserted ally when he dropped some money then bent to pick it up.

She snuck up behind him, her disguise still firmly in place. "Are you all right?" she asked innocently.

He looked her up and down then his gaze lingered on her chest. "Ah, yeah. I guess so. Can I help you with something?"

"Oh, I was just near and saw you struggling to hold on to your money. Usually people keep it in banks, don't they?"

"Yeah, well, this won't be going there. I won it fair and square. Not sharing it with anyone. I'm Levi." He stuck his stubby hand out for her to shake.

"I have two names, but you can call me Angel." She smiled at him. Her teeth were slightly pointed, but other than that, she still looked human enough.

"That's a pretty name. Wanna come have a few drinks with me and my mum?" He shuffled on one foot then quickly glanced at her, relaxing when she smiled.

"Sure, I'd love that." She motioned for him to lead.

They walked for maybe twenty minutes until they reached a tiny flat with string lights around the poles of a carport and crisscrossing the roof. The multicoloured lights flashed, and music blared from a crackly speaker.

An older-looking woman was glaring at the screen of her phone, a drink in one hand. Humans were so strange. "You stupid piece of crap, I'll smash your face." She looked up then, and stared open-mouthed at Angel. She had her son's misshapen features, and the same slow look. How odd.

Angel cocked her head slightly and smiled in genuine amusement. These creatures were darker than the other humans. They would make good pets, but she would tire of them easily enough.

"Oh, hey. Didn't realise Levi brought a friend home.

Refugees

Was just going off at his ex. Goddamn snow queen keeps taking all his money." She took another large gulp of the poison in her hand.

Angel lashed out quickly, hitting Levi in the head, knocking him unconscious then turned to his mother, who was staring in horror with her mouth hanging open. Angel sauntered deliberately towards the old lady, letting her disguise slip enough that she would know what her true face looked like.

"You're pathetic. You think paper and poison are important. There's so much more happening in this universe than that, and here you are, filled with toxins and living in squalid conditions." Her eyes flickered to the messy room behind the mother for a moment.

"So what, you working for the snow queen now?" she snapped.

Angel didn't know who this snow queen was, but she was curious. Why was she called that and what did she do to get the title? Then she was intent again, the fleeting curiosity vanishing as quickly as it had come. Angel sized the woman up and decided to get rid of her quickly. Levi was stirring, and she had bigger plans for him. She launched forwards and grabbed the older woman in a tight hug, squeezing until she heard bones crack, one hand on her mouth so she didn't scream loudly. She then dragged her into the messy house and closed all the curtains, excitement building in her.

The strange woman wasn't dead yet, but she was incapable of moving now. Angel snarled her pleasure viciously and went to retrieve Levi. She flung him into a chair and bound him with a nearby garland left over from some party. Then she propped his mother up so she could watch her son. This was always the fun part. The mother's injuries were mortal, but she would live long enough to see this.

Angel clawed his face, and he screamed. Blood gushed down his neck and onto his shirt, splattering the floor and walls as he thrashed. His teeth were visible through the gashes. She liked that. It gave him a hideous look that she found funny. His eyes had been closed, but after a few minutes, he opened them and looked at her stupidly then he saw his mother.

"Mom! What the hell did you do?" he bellowed.

Angel smiled, showing all her pointed teeth, and didn't answer. She seized a nearby bat, testing it on the mother first then hit Levi as hard as she could in the knee. The force of the blow left an indent in his leg and it instantly turned purple and swelled. She snarled, amused, enjoying his screams. His mother watched and whimpered helplessly. Her anguish made Angel feel more powerful.

She turned her attention back to Levi, who'd stopped screaming. He was still sobbing, though, and she considered him for a minute. What should she do to him? How could she hurt him the most without killing him yet? She didn't have access to Ashan root here, so she needed to be careful and not cause so much internal damage that he couldn't survive or stay conscious. She kicked and punched him then when that palled, she moved onto burning. Using a lighter she found on a nearby table, she lit a fire in a wastepaper bin and used the flames to make a brand, using a golf club she'd spied nearby. She tore his shirt open and branded him near his collar bones and sternum, moving down his torso onto his limbs. She was careful to reheat the makeshift brand so it stayed red hot, and his screams intensified with each new burn.

His mother screamed, a strangled sound, so Angel burned her as well, mostly on her face and neck, and when she

Refugees

passed out after about three hours, her face lost its colour. She was clearly about to die, which would ruin Angel's fun. She grabbed a hunting knife she'd found in one of the rooms and stabbed Levi with it a few times. He seemed not to even feel the pain now, and it was starting to get boring. She yanked his head backwards and slit his throat, one swift and deep cut, then watched as he took his last breaths. His face was prettier this way. It was swollen and covered in bruises and gashes. It was art, and she decided whimsically to arrange both him and his mother in a display fit for a shamed Huntowra, sprawling out their mangled bodies grotesquely for all to admire, or fear. Then she left the mother to gasp her last breaths all alone, while staring at what was left of her son.

Angel had nowhere to go. The A.S.U wasn't an option now. She would have to find a dimensional soft spot and force her way through to the nearest world with magix. This world was problematic, and the humans needed to be exterminated. Despite not having magix, this horrid species was a massive threat, and she wanted them gone…permanently. She wandered aimlessly in the dark, not paying attention to where she was until Bryant jumped out from nowhere and tackled her to the ground. She fought hard, trying to escape him, but he was stronger than she'd realised. He was also a much better tracker than she'd given him credit for. Stupid Talgra. She should've killed him in his sleep.

* * * *

Bryant was happy he'd found her so quickly. He'd thought it would take longer. This was a large planet, and she could've gone anywhere to hide. When he stood up, he noticed she was covered in blood, and it now smeared his hands and clothes where he'd tackled her.

The blood drained from his face. Damn, she'd hurt someone already. That was fast. He hadn't expected that, and now it was his fault someone was badly hurt...or worse. He pulled out his phone and dialled his brother.

"Hey, it's me. I got her, but not before she got someone else."

He listened a minute then made a humph sound and clicked the phone off, tucking it back into the pocket of his pants. After taking a deep breath, he rolled his shoulders and hoisted Angel up over them and made his way back to A.S.U.

Chapter 40

The day of the ball was here, and Jayne was still working on her mask. She'd been having strange dreams since her healing sessions began, though physically she felt much better. Her gown was already done, but the shoes were wrong so she was going to her mother's to get a silver strappy pair of flats instead. Her mother and Dae had been oddly quiet, and she couldn't help the strange, paranoid feeling that she was being talked about, though she tried to ignore it. If it was important, they would talk to her.

Dae was still out on a mission, so her mother was collecting her today, but Dae would be back in time for tonight's ball. He was her date. She'd wanted to ask Peter, but as he was considered royalty, he was going with the royal family, though he'd assured her they would see each other at the ball. She flipped the sign on the door to closed and locked up, grabbing her beading basket on the way to the back room. She cleaned up a little until her mother pulled up and beeped the horn. She grabbed her stuff and dashed out, slamming the door behind her.

"Hey, Mama," she said with a childlike giggle.

"Well, you're fired up again today, love. Still feeling good?"

Jayne nodded with enthusiasm. She hummed the whole car ride, her mother smiling gently but not speaking.

When they got to the house, Jayne raced in through the

back door and up the stairs to her mother's bedroom. She yanked open the cupboard and started pulling out assorted boxes and baskets until she reached the shoe box she was searching for. A quick glance showed her the shoes were perfect so she set them aside to put everything else away. She was careful now and looked curiously at her mother's belongings. There was an old doll, her hair and dress like nothing Jayne had ever seen before, and a box with some clothes bundled up and thrown into a plastic bag.

After checking that her mother wasn't near, she pulled them out to get a closer look. She gasped. There was a woman's outfit and a child's, and both were bloodstained and damaged. Underneath these, there was a child-sized sword of bright silver with a gold strip down the centre. Symbols were engraved in the golden parts and around the hilt, and there was one in the handle that reminded her of her dream, though this was more detailed. The gemstone set into the hilt was similar to amethyst, yet it was paler and had tiny gold flecks throughout. It was so pretty she could barely believe her eyes, and she felt oddly attached to it.

With the sword was a sheath made from a strange leather, very ornate with another symbol on it. She'd seen it somewhere before, she just couldn't place where. Finally, there were her clothes from when she was found. This box must contain clothes that had some significance to Ashlyn; Jayne would have to ask her about it all one day.

She packed it all back into the box and put it away but kept the sword and sheath out. On her way out of the closet, she tripped on a basket she hadn't noticed before. It brimmed with beautiful flowers, in many colours, and apples. Why would her mother have apples and flowers in her closet? Then she saw

217

Refugees

something else in the basket: an etched glass dome—which contained an infinity clock and a plaque she couldn't read at a distance—and a dagger, wrapped loosely in a tan cloth.

Jayne knelt and gently lifted the dagger. It was stunning. The casing was bronze with gold accents and some kind of gemstones she didn't recognise. They made a picture of an ancient dragon with amber eyes. She felt a tingle and her mind wandered for a second before she placed it to the side so she could get the clock out. She gently turned it around, looking at the image on the glass, which showed several childlike faces. A small set of gemstones had been placed on either side of the clock's hands to keep them from moving. It was gorgeous and fascinating, and the lights of the room made the faces dance and shimmer as though they were alive. Then she read the inscription on the front.

Troy Hastings, hero of Helios, for incredible bravery and courage.

This was Ashlyn's husband. Whenever they spoke of him, it was always vague and short-lived, but this plaque said he was a hero. She'd known he'd died in a war, but she hadn't known he'd been honoured for his services. Nor had she heard of a place called Helios.

Jayne heard shuffling on the stairs and quickly put everything back and slammed the door shut just as her mother came in.

"Okay, love? Did you find the shoes?" Then she saw the dagger and sword, and she sighed, a look of resignation coming over her face.

Jayne blushed and shrugged as she bent over to pick them up and hugged them to her body, not really knowing why.

"Yeah, I did, thanks. Can I finish making the mask here and change when it's time? Dae won't be back until the ball's started so Eva's picking me up."

Ashlyn's face drained, and she looked dizzy for a minute.

Jayne jumped up and rushed to her. "Oh my god, Mama, are you okay?"

"Yeah, I'm okay. Actually, I need to tell you something. Can we sit a minute while you finish the mask?"

Jayne smiled and nodded then curled up on the foot of her mother's bed, set the sword and dagger down, and beaded the wires in between the eyes of the mask. She'd been dreaming of wings and wanted to recreate the design for tonight. She was wearing her hair down tonight. No wigs or contacts, just herself. She decided to also wear the sword and dagger. It seemed somehow appropriate.

Her mother was playing with wisps of her hair. "So, I had a chat with your brother the other day, and now I want to tell you something. It's a bit of a secret, though, and with Evaliah coming here, I'll need your help to keep it. Can you help me, honey? It's really important."

"Sure." Jayne nodded. "Hey, why did you call her that? I didn't know you knew her full name." She frowned a little but kept working.

"Well, I've met Eva before, actually. We were friends, but she thinks I died, a very long time ago in another place. If some people found out I wasn't dead, they would send terrible people after us, to kill us. So, when she gets here, I can't see her. She can't know I'm here, Jayne. Can you promise me you won't say anything?" Ashlyn looked at her daughter seriously.

Refugees

"Okay, but I think you owe me an explanation." Jayne looked hard at her mother.

Ashlyn sighed and nodded then patted Jayne's shoulder. "Okay, we can talk about everything after the ball." She dropped her gaze to the mask in Jayne's lap. "That mask looks amazing now. Kind of similar to the sword, actually."

The wings were finished, and they kind of reminded her of a dragon's eye. Jayne jumped up and rushed to get ready for tonight. The gown was a shimmery white, floor-length and fitted with a small train that feathered out and a slit up one side to the thigh. There were several accents that resembled brooches holding the fabric together. The dress showed some cleavage with a dip in the front, and had an overcoat of lace that gave it a vintage feel.

Jayne left her hair loose but added a white bejewelled butterfly comb at the last minute, scraping a small section of hair from each side of her face back and securing it at the back of her head. She wound the wires of the mask into her hair and tied them underneath, so the ties weren't visible. With the mask, she wouldn't need shadow or mascara, so she simply added lip-gloss, deciding that her milky skin didn't need any makeup. It was a natural look, which she rarely liked. She popped on the strappy shoes, then, on some strange instinct, added the sheathed sword, tying it around her waist. The sword tilted to her left, though she was right-handed, but that was fine with her. It wasn't like she would use it. She tucked the dagger into the front of the sheath, using the small chain on the end of the dagger to secure it then went down to wait with her mother, who gasped and started crying at the sight of her.

"You look exquisite, Kitty. I'm feeling a little speechless. Are you sure you can keep the secret, about what I said before?"

Jayne nodded and gave her a small smile but there was no time to reply before there was a loud knocking on the door. Ashlyn wiped a tear and looked at her quickly again then left the room hurriedly. Jayne took a deep breath, making sure her mother was gone before she opened the door. She was shocked to see Seth there instead of Eva. She blinked in surprise, and he chuckled.

"Sorry, Jayne, I guess nobody called you. Eva is busy at the moment. There was a…situation. So I'm here to drive you to the ball. You ready?" He gestured at her gown, and she nodded, following him out into the evening.

Refugees

Chapter 41

Jayne was a bundle of nerves, and it showed. The entire car ride, she was twisting her hands and fidgeting like a child on a sugar high.

Seth barked out an abrupt laugh, his eyes crinkled with genuine amusement. "Sorry. It's just you're so fidgety. Guess you're feeling anxious, huh?"

He didn't seem to want an actual response, but she still thought about it. "I guess I am, though I don't know why, really. Hey, look at this. My mom gave me this sword and dagger today. Well, they were already mine, but they were hidden from me until now. I don't remember where I got them from or anything, I just feel excited to have them." She shrugged then, a small gesture, and he nodded in understanding, glancing at her sword and dagger with sharp eyes.

She wondered why but was too nervous to ask.

It was a quick drive, and she wasn't surprised to see they'd arrived already, but she was shocked at the carpark. It looked so different now, with Starling Trumpets lining the road, making it look like you were driving through tunnels of the plants, and someone had entwined twinkling soft lights through the whole thing. There had to be thousands of them.

"Wow," she gasped almost inaudibly, and Seth murmured in agreement.

They were guided into a parking space then made their way to the entrance. The giant doors stood open, and the decorations continued inside. It was a seamless transition, and the stone floors glimmered with the twinkling lights above. They turned to the right and headed to the far door, but instead of going through it, they went upstairs via a hidden stairway that led to the main staircase in the enormous meeting room they were using for the ball tonight. Probably to allow the guests to enter with flare.

When they approached the stairs, Damian was waiting. He was dressed in a formal tux, with his hair pushed back off his face, leaving the scar he'd gotten in the accident that had killed their mother starkly visible.

Seth quietly left to find Jye and left them to enter on their own.

"This is my favourite dress up, Kitty," he said, giving her a cheeky grin and a wink.

She giggled. "Thanks, I like yours too, Dae. Wanna go to a party? We got all dressed up and stuff."

He grinned at her and offered his arm with a giant wave and bow…like in the olden-day movies she loved so much.

She curtseyed and took the arm, and together they started down the staircase.

They were about halfway down when people noticed them. It took a minute to realise everyone was stopping in their tracks and staring open-mouthed at them. Jayne slowed, anxiety fluttering the pulse in her neck, and Damian squeezed her hand. There was some uncertainty in his eyes as well, but smiled gamely, so she did the same.

* * * *

Peter was talking with Matt and Jess when the murmur

Refugees

of the crowd seemed to fall away. Matt must've noticed too, because he stopped talking about the wards they were trying to repair and leaned round Peter's enormous frame to see why everyone was going silent. He paled abruptly, swaying, then dropped his glass of whiskey and let out a strangled noise that might've been a cry.

Peter turned rapidly on the spot, expecting an attack, then froze in the middle of the room. Her. She was here, but how, and why? How? His breathing stopped and his arms were limp by his sides. His eyes felt like they were about to burst into flames. The symbol on her mask, her flowing locks… She was so very tiny. Then he looked into her eyes, pure green fire, and he slipped away from the world. Everything went black and his head registered a sharp pain before…nothing.

"What the hell happened to him?" Emma said in a sharp voice.

He opened his eyes. Emma was hovering over him, and Hannah was holding his head, which was tingling again. He'd collapsed.

And then he remembered why. He looked right at Emma and almost cried, "Lilah, she's here." Her face went slack then she spun, searching the room.

"Oh my god," was all she said, her hands at her mouth to stifle her sobs. She seemed unable to move, except for the uncontrollable shaking.

Peter sat up slowly. There were people all around, but nobody was moving. Lilah was still standing there like an angel. Finally, Peter found his way up to his feet. He took a breath in then slowly raised his eyes to her again, careful now.

She looked terrified. Her teeth worried at her bottom lip,

which trembled, and she was clutching Damian's hand. It hit him. Damian, he was her biological brother. He was Daemon. And she was Lilah... His Lilah. Fury washed over him for a second and the ground shook before he regained control. He wanted to go to her, but the intensity of his emotions concerned him. He needed a minute.

Just then, an unnatural screeching sound came from behind them. A blur flashed past Peter, headed right for Lilah. Her arms came up in front of her face defensively, and the blur grabbed her and spun around, just as a powerful burst of energy exploded all round them, flinging them both into the magix ring. The shields came up and the binding symbols he'd drawn earlier activated. Chains sprung up all around Angel, binding her, digging into her flesh, and snaking around her neck and wings to prevent her from trying to use them.

She was hissing and growling at Lilah, who was knocked to the floor in the magix circle. The floor shook, and a loud rumbling started all round. Lilah tried to move but she was stuck. The circle wouldn't allow her to leave. It glowed, and her symbol formed above as it had the first time. A lullaby began, softly at first then growing louder. Just when they thought it was stopping, a bolt of lightning struck the ring, hitting Lilah, and she collapsed. The power bands lit up, visible for the first time. They were woven into her flesh. Whatever had happened had buried them inside her body.

He looked at Matt and saw his horror reflected on the emperor's face. This would kill her, and soon. Then he felt a tugging on his left wrist, and the eternal bracelet that linked them was visible again. The chain was connected to them both and he saw with horror that the power band on his arm, the one he put there to stop the pain, was sucking magix from her.

Refugees

"Crap," he muttered, angry at himself.

He yanked the band off and it instantly stopped sucking magix, but she wasn't waking. He was thinking so fast, he felt dizzy again. One thought ran into the next with no time for him to consider the answers. Was she too weak? Did she need to eat some of the berries? He could bring the tree here... He'd have to show them, but she was more important than the secret they'd kept. He made his mind up in an instant then stepped forwards and braced himself.

Everyone was looking at her, so he drew his fist back and then punched a hole right through the barriers and stepped into the magix square. Some people were shouting, but he wasn't listening now. He needed to help her, and he needed to focus to do that. He flung out his arms in either direction, and a wave of energy shot out of his hands in a shower of sparks. It billowed out to the edges of the square and rebuilt the barriers, which silenced the entire room. He knew why. It wasn't possible to break them in the first place, and now he'd unbroken them too.

At this point, there was nothing left to hide, so he let his magix flow into him fully. It changed the tux he'd worn to the ball into a warrior's pants and a vest, along with a cloak that was nothing like anything anyone had seen before. Her symbol was woven into the fabric at the back, and the metal clasp at his neck was the same emblem. He had a crown of circles on his head and more arm bands than anyone he'd ever known. They denoted a warrior's rank and power status, and Peter's bands covered his whole upper arms, almost like armour. A fine chink sound reached him, and the sheathed sword she wore magicked to him. Mirren. He'd missed his companion and magicked it into place across his shoulders.

He gathered his strength and let magix flow from him into the space surrounding the green circle. The barriers he'd just restored strained, and he worried they wouldn't hold up under the force of his magix. He focused again, visualising the berry tree and its fruit. The floor cracked, letting the new tree form. As it grew, it leaned over slightly as though it wanted to hug Lilah while she slept, and the lullaby continued.

The tree matured and fruited within ten minutes. Glowing with energy, they fell to the floor before exploding into silver ribbons of energy that headed straight to her. Her body absorbed the life force, and she stirred, not yet awake but strong enough now to survive what was coming next. He would too. He knew because he'd done the same thing when he'd been sent to the Qualterra by accident the first time. He'd blown apart.

She must have too from whatever the Five had done to her, and the result was that the power bands had embedded themselves in her body and were sucking her life away. No wonder she'd been so sick, and why she'd always insisted on hiding. Subconsciously, she had to have been terrified of what she'd been through and acted accordingly. He knew what to do. The tree would remain, and they would both recover, but this would hurt like hell.

He went to her then and looked at Matt. Her father nodded once, a tear glistening in his eye, but he didn't look away. The entire room held their breath, not knowing what was happening. Mirren was bouncing on his feet with huge eyes, twisting his hands in front of him. Peter built up an enormous amount of energy then set it loose in the tiny circle. It had nowhere to go so it exploded, as intended. The bands released, and he vanished them in the second before he blew apart as

Refugees

well.

* * * *

"Are they awake yet?" An impatient voice reached Peter's ears, and he wished he wasn't.

He didn't want to have this conversation yet, not with his mother. She sounded like an angry cat, almost hissing underneath the anxiety.

"Not yet, Milly. I'll let you know when he wakes. You might want to go easy. He did just explode, after all," Eva said dryly.

Milly's footsteps retreated, and he sighed and opened his eyes. He looked over at Sam, who was watching his mother stalk away angrily with a frown. Eva was at the next bed over, tending to Lilah, and she smiled at him when she saw he was awake. She put her finger to her mouth to shush him and went back to what she was doing. He felt grateful that she was letting him rest some more before his mother murdered him. He looked at Lilah now. She looked better. There were pink spots on her cheeks and her skin seemed less wax-like, though still very pale.

She was sleeping, and he wondered if she was dreaming. She was such an odd little creature… He smiled. Odd, yes, and also half of him.

P. Ryall

About the Author

P. Ryall began writing as a way to share stories with her children, and discovered she has a passion for it. Her debut novel is part of a planned series, The Magix Series, and she has already released a short story set in this world. *The Fall of the Aggaron* was a limited release short story that will be extended into a short novel, the prequel to *Refugees*. She plans to create an anthology of short stories in the future and make them available everywhere

www.ingramcontent.com/pod-product-compliance
Lightning Source LLC
Chambersburg PA
CBHW052021070526
44584CB00016B/1853